Deadly Women
Volume One

18 Shocking
True Murder Cases

Robert Keller

**Please Leave Your Review of This Book At
http://bit.ly/kellerbooks**

ISBN-13: 978-1976066924

ISBN-10: 1976066921

© 2017 by Robert Keller

robertkellerauthor.com

Table of Contents

Omaima Aree Nelson

Like every other man on the premises, Bill Nelson had noticed the woman the minute she'd walked into the bar. She was petite, dark-haired and beautiful, definitely out of his league. Now, however, she was standing close by, watching intently as he lined up a shot at the pool table. Several of the local studs had already tried talking to her and had been promptly rebuffed, but when Bill looked up and made eye contact with the woman, she gave him a demure smile. Bill felt his pulse race. Could she really be interested in him?

Eventually, Bill felt he had to try his luck. He walked over and introduced himself. Dark eyes sparkling, the young woman extended a tiny hand. Her name was Omaima, she said, in an accent that only added to her allure.

Bill and Omaima spent the rest of that evening, October 23, 1991, filling each other in on their respective backgrounds. He told her that he was a retired airline pilot. She said that she was an aspiring model who was working as a nanny to make ends meet. Omaima's accent and dark good looks were also explained. Egyptian-born, the 24-year-old had come to the United States in 1986, hoping for a better life. Then Omaima confided something that got Bill flustered all over again. She preferred older men, she said, particularly if they were tall. At 56 years of age and standing 6-foot-4, Bill qualified on both counts. They left the bar together that night, driving to Bill Nelson's luxury Costa Mesa apartment in his red Corvette. Within days, Bill had proposed and Omaima had gleefully accepted.

William E. Nelson was a man of the world and should have known better. There was a lot that he didn't know about his new bride. He did not know, for example, that Omaima had a history of irrational and violent behavior; he did not know that he was far from the first "older man" she'd seduced, nor that her previous conquests had ended up shackled to their beds, pistol-whipped and robbed of their money and valuables. Bill was too busy enjoying the attention of his beautiful, young wife to concern himself with such things. Omaima was a skilled and adventurous lover. When she suggested introducing bondage into their sex games, Bill willingly agreed.

So it was that on November 28, 1991, Bill Nelson ended up shackled to his bed with his wife straddling him. Breathlessly anticipating the sex that was to come, he failed to notice when Omaima reached down to grasp a pair of scissors. By the time she lifted the weapon and held it above her head, two-handed, it was too late. Bill barely had time to utter a sound before the twin blades plunged into his chest.

The attack was prolonged and continued even after Bill Nelson was dead. In addition to the scissor attack, he was bludgeoned repeatedly with a domestic iron. Finally, exhausted, Omaima slumped forward against her husband's battered and bloodied body, her breath coming in short, rapid gasps. She held that position for only a moment. There was work to do, a corpse to be disposed of.

Getting rid of a human body is a lot more difficult in practice than it appears in principal. William Nelson was a large man, standing over 6 feet tall and weighing in at 230 pounds. Still, Omaima was nothing if not determined. Over the hours that followed, she decapitated, dismembered, and disemboweled her husband's corpse. Some of the body parts were ground down in the garbage disposal. Others were packed into suitcases and placed in the back seat of Bill's Corvette.

But Omaima did not discard all of Bill's remains. Choice cuts were held back, broiled, breaded and deep-fried. Then Omaima sat down at the dinner table and enjoyed her feast, liberally coating the macabre cutlets in barbecue sauce. Later, she would joke to police, "Nothing tastes as good as the man I married. It's the sauce that does it."

The murder of William Nelson was not a well thought out crime. As the surviving spouse, Omaima would immediately have come under suspicion once Bill's disappearance was noticed. And the amount of blood and tissue left at the crime scene would have been a CSI's idea of nirvana. However, Omaima hastened her own downfall by involving others in the murder. Uncertain of what to do with the rest of Bill's remains, she began visiting ex-boyfriends, asking for help. One of them went to the police.

Detectives were soon pounding on the door of the Nelsons' Costa Mesa apartment. Inside, they found a scene of utter carnage. There was blood spattered on the walls, pooled on the floor and soaked into the mattress. Plastic bags held crudely hacked chunks of flesh and gristle. Bill's boiled head was in the refrigerator, flesh falling away from the skull. His hands floated in the deep fryer, partially cooked. In the back of the Corvette were two suitcases, each containing hacked flesh and coils of viscera. When the coroner's office weighed the accumulated body parts, 80 pounds of William Nelson was unaccounted for.

Omaima Nelson was placed under arrest and charged with murder. She made no attempt to deny that she'd killed her husband but insisted that she had acted in self-defense. She said that Bill had been intolerably cruel to her, had beaten, choked and bitten her. She said that he'd tied her to the bed and raped her on numerous occasions. She'd acted out of self-preservation, she said.

But that did not explain the horrendous mutilations, nor the acts of cannibalism that she'd admitted to. Omaima had a ready explanation. She said that after killing Bill she'd fallen into a "trance-like state." She had no recollection of hacking him up, although she did recall cutting off his penis. That, she claimed, must have been an "unconscious act of revenge" for a rape she'd suffered in childhood.

The prosecutor wasn't buying Omaima Nelson's self-defense argument and Omaima hardly helped herself when she told a court-appointed psychiatrist that her husband's ribs were, "so sweet, so delicious... I like mine tender."

Tried and found guilty of murder in February 1993, Omaima Nelson was sentenced to 28 years to life. She is currently incarcerated at the Central California Women's Facility in Chowchilla. Parole applications in 2006 and 2011 were both denied. She becomes eligible again in 2026.

Susan Smith

At around 9 p.m. on the evening of Tuesday, October 24, 1994, Shirley McCloud was relaxing in the living room of her home in Union, South Carolina. She'd just put aside that day's edition of the local newspaper, the Union Daily Times, when there was a commotion outside. Shirley turned on the porch light and peered through the drapes. A young woman stood on the porch. "Please help me!" she wailed. "He's got my kids!" Shirley then opened the door and ushered the woman inside, while her son dialed 911.

A Union County Deputy was dispatched to the McCloud house immediately. There, the distraught woman identified herself as Susan Smith and told her story. She said that she'd been driving her car with her two young sons, Michael, 3, and Alex, 14 months, in the back. She'd stopped at a red light at the Monarch Mills intersection when a black man had suddenly wrenched the door open, got in and told her to drive. Four miles out of town he'd instructed her to pull over at a spot near John D. Long Lake. There, he'd produced a gun and forced her from the vehicle. He'd then raced away with the two boys still in the back. Frantic, Susan had run to the nearest house, the McCloud's, which stood about a quarter mile from the lake.

By now, Union County Sheriff Howard Wells had been alerted to the abduction and had arrived at the McCloud residence. He asked Susan to repeat her story and then decided to call in the South Carolina Law Enforcement Division (SLED).

But already an element of doubt had begun to surface regarding Susan Smith's story. The traffic light at the junction where she claimed the carjacking had occurred was set permanently on green. It only turned red if a car was approaching from the other direction. In other words, if Susan had stopped at a red light, there must have been another driver there who would have witnessed the abduction. Nothing had thus far been reported.

Sherriff Wells noted the discrepancy but at this point, he filed it away. His immediate priority was to find the missing toddlers. That operation was now in full swing, with a SLED helicopter scouring the nearby Sumter National Forest and divers searching the murky waters of John D. Long Lake. Meanwhile, a description of Susan's burgundy Mazda Protégé had been circulated and Susan was working with a police sketch artist to draw up a composite of the kidnapper.

In the days that followed, the search was intensified and expanded. The case was already garnering media attention far beyond the backwater of Union, South Carolina. It was now national news and there was an outpouring of sympathy for Susan Smith and her estranged husband David, as they appeared on radio and television to appeal for the safe return of their children.

In between those media appearances, Susan and David were interviewed by several law enforcement agencies. In addition to the Union County Sheriff's Department and SLED, the FBI had been called into the investigation. On   Thursday, October 27, they administered polygraphs to both David and Susan Smith. David's results indicated that he knew nothing about the disappearance of his sons. Susan's was inconclusive. Her response to the question: "Do you know where your children are?" drew particular attention.

As the investigation continued, detectives began to pick up a number of inconsistencies in Susan Smith's testimony. In addition to the mistake she'd made about the intersection where the abduction had supposedly occurred, there were discrepancies about where she'd been going on the night her children were taken. Initially, she said she'd been on her way to visit a friend.

When that turned out to be a lie, she said she'd driven to the local Wal-Mart. Finally, she said that she'd just driven around aimlessly. She'd kept that from the police, she explained, because it would have sounded "suspicious."

Investigators were by now sure that Susan was not telling everything that she knew. When they learned that her boyfriend Tom Findlay had recently broken off their relationship because he didn't want the responsibility of her sons, they quizzed her about it. "No man would make me hurt my children," Susan said. "They were my life." Detectives couldn't help noticing that she referred to her sons in the past tense.

Then, after SLED Agent David A. Caldwell pressed her about the inconsistencies in her story, she responded angrily. "You son of a bitch! How can you think that! I can't believe that you think I did it!" She then burst out crying. Agent Caldwell would later remark that although she made sobbing sounds, there were no tears in her eyes.

On the third day of the investigation, divers were again sent to the depths of
John D. Long Lake, sticking close to the shoreline where they believed a submerged vehicle might have settled. They found nothing. On Friday, October 28, four days since the abduction, fifty

volunteer firefighters and dozens of police officers searched the woods near the lake. They too came up empty.

Officers had by now decided that Susan Smith was involved in the disappearance of her children. They did not believe necessarily that she'd killed the boys. Susan was in the midst of a messy divorce from her husband. The police suspected that she'd hidden the children somewhere in order to circumvent custody issues.

The decision was then made to increase the pressure on Susan. She was subjected to a coordinated daily roster of interrogations, with many of the investigators stating openly that they believed she was lying about her involvement in the disappearances. But Susan Smith was tougher than any of them had anticipated. She continued to protest her innocence.

On Thursday, November 3, 1995, the ninth day since the abduction, Susan and David Smith appeared on CBS This Morning. Susan was asked directly if she had any involvement in the disappearance of her sons. She responded by saying, "I did not have anything to do with the abduction of my children. Whoever did this is a sick and emotionally unstable person."

That same afternoon Susan was again interrogated by Sheriff Wells, the interview taking place at the Family Center of the First Baptist Church. Wells told her that he knew her story about the

black carjacker was a lie and that he was going to have to release
that fact to the news media, because her accusation was causing
unrest in Union's black community. Susan then asked Wells to
pray with her. At the conclusion of the prayers she broke down
and started crying, repeating over and over "I'm so ashamed." She
then began telling Wells what had really happened on the night of
October 25.

Susan said that she'd been driving around with her sons in the car,
trying to calm herself down. She was feeling lonely and depressed,
overwhelmed by the problems in her life. She and her husband
David were in the midst of a divorce. She'd also been abandoned
by her lover Tom Findlay, who'd sent her a letter that day ending
their relationship. She wanted to end her life but she didn't want
her children to suffer by being left on their own after she was
gone. She'd therefore decided to kill them too.

After driving around for an hour, she'd found herself at John D.
Long Lake. She'd then driven to the lake's seventy-five-foot boat
ramp and parked in the middle of it. She sat behind the wheel
contemplating what she was going to do next, while her sons slept
in the back, strapped into their car seats.

After a while, she shifted the vehicle into neutral and allowed it to
roll down the boat ramp. But it had traveled only a short distance

when she pulled the handbrake. Then she got out of the car and stood on the ramp, looking down at the dark waters of the lake.

Susan Smith has never been able to adequately explain her next action. She leaned into the car and released the brake. Then she stood and watched as the vehicle rolled down the ramp and entered the water. It did not sink immediately but bobbed on the surface, drifting away from the shore, slowly filling with water. Then it disappeared under the water, carrying her two young boys to their deaths.

The trial of Susan Smith began on July 19, 1995. The prosecution, led by Union County Solicitor Thomas Pope, stated its intention up front. They wanted the death penalty for a woman who'd callously murdered her two sons in order to win back her lover. David Bruck, appearing for the defense, told a different story, the story of a lonely, clinically depressed and deeply troubled woman who had a history of suicide attempts and had acted out of absolute helplessness.

The trial threw up plenty of other sensational headlines, not least involving Susan Smith's convoluted love life. At the time she murdered her sons, she was sexually involved with four men, including her estranged husband, her stepfather, and the father of her boyfriend.

In the end, the jury returned the guilty verdict that the prosecution wanted but decided against the death penalty. Susan Smith was sentenced to life in prison. She will be eligible for parole in 2025, when she will be 53 years old.

Tillie Klimek

Otillie "Tillie" Gburek was born in Poland in 1876, and came to the United States as a child, settling with her parents amongst the large Polish community on Chicago's Near North Side. There, Tillie grew to be a plain-looking girl with a squat, beefy physique and a somewhat short temper. She was certainly no catch but it appears that she had no shortage of suitors as a young woman. In 1892, aged just 16, she accepted a proposal from one of them.

John Mitkiewicz was by all accounts a good husband to Tillie, a hard-working, salt-of-the-earth type of fellow who did not look too deeply into the vodka bottle and didn't chase other women. Their marriage was, by all accounts, a happy one, surviving twenty years of domestic mundanity unscathed. Then, in 1914, something changed. Tillie began to complain of experiencing terrifying visions of her husband's imminent death. So lucid were these visualizations that she could name the exact day that John Mitkiewicz would pass into the hereafter.

Of course, no one took Tillie seriously. They told her that she was probably experiencing the effects of early onset menopause. But then John did fall ill and, sure enough, he died on the date that Tillie had predicted. "A coincidence," Tillie's friends and family assured her, although Tillie remained convinced that she'd somehow gained the power of foretelling. She put aside her grief just long enough to call on the insurance company to collect on John's life policy.

Tillie was now forty years old and a widow. She'd never been a beauty to begin with and time had not improved her looks. Friends were concerned that she'd live out her days lonely and alone but they'd made an improper assessment of Tillie's charms. Within two months of her husband's death, she was dating again, stepping out with a strapping laborer named John Ruskowski. Soon Ruskowski had proposed and Tillie had accepted. But then came those pesky visions again, telling her that her husband's days were numbered. Within six months of wedding Tillie, Ruskowski fell ill. He died on the exact date that Tillie had predicted. Fortunately, her visions had given her the foresight to take out a policy on his life.

You might have thought that with the troubling visions predicting the demise of her nearest and dearest, Tillie would have been scared off the dating game by now. Not so. She was soon back in the saddle again. But then the man she'd set her sights on changed his mind and dumped her. Understandably upset, Tillie consoled herself with the fact that she'd seen his imminent death in a vision. And, as always, she was correct. The faithless lover died as predicted, even if Tillie's date of death was a few days out this time.

Tillie's next conquest was a man named Frank Kupszcyk. No sooner had the ink dried on their marriage certificate than Tillie was telling neighbors: "He won't last long." So confident was she of Frank's imminent death, in fact, that she bought a budget coffin and asked her landlord if she could store it in the basement. Then she got to work knitting the mourning cap she intended wearing to Frank's funeral.

Sure enough, Frank fell ill with similar symptoms to those that had afflicted Tillie's former husbands. "It won't be long now," Tillie assured him. And it wasn't. Frank Kupszcyk died on the exact day that Tillie had predicted. So too did Tillie's fourth husband, Joseph Guszkowski. He'd scoffed at the warnings of his friends and family, calling them superstitious nonsense. But whether he believed in Tillie's ghoulish predictive powers on not, the Reaper knocked on his door precisely when Tillie said he would. Guszkowski's death heralded another predictable outcome, too. A fat insurance check landed in Tillie's bank account.

Tillie's predictions of death had by now earned her an ominous reputation in her neighborhood. People would cross the street when they saw her coming, afraid that they might somehow be touched by the angel of death. And their fears were not without foundation. Aside from the four husbands she'd already dispatched, other people in Tillie's circle were dying too. Three members of a family she'd quarreled with had died in agony after she'd predicted their deaths; her ex-boyfriend, Joseph Grantkowski, had died after jilting her; four of Tillie's cousins had expired after being attended by her; several members of the Koulik family – into which Tillie's cousin Nellie had married – had become ill and had succumbed to mysterious ailments. There were others too, usually people who'd annoyed Tillie in some or other minor way, or from whose death she could benefit.

With all of this going on, it is a wonder that Tillie was still able to attract suitors. Yet she was. Next up was Anton Klimek, who proposed to Tillie in 1921, over the objections of his family. No sooner had he bequeathed all of his worldly possessions to his new bride than he was struck down by a sudden and debilitating illness.

This time, however, Tillie had met her match. Her in-laws had been prepared for just such an outcome and they arrived en masse to spirit Anton away to the hospital. There, under the care of medical staff, he made a full recovery, thus ruining Tillie's near perfect record as a harbinger of death. That, however, was the least of her problems. The Klimek's insisted that doctors test Anton's blood, hair and fingernails for traces of arsenic and it was via these tests that the mystery of Tillie's predictive powers was finally unraveled. Anton's samples showed positive for the poison. His family wasted little time in taking the findings to the police.

Tillie Klimek was taken into custody that same day, along with her cousin, Nellie Koulik, who police believed had been her accomplice. Under questioning the women remained steadfast in their denials but it was only a matter of time before the truth was revealed. Tillie's former husbands had all been exhumed for postmortem. The results would prove that each of the men had died of arsenic poisoning.

Tillie Klimek was brought to trial in March 1923, charged with only one murder, that of her third husband, Frank Kupzsyk. Found guilty on that charge, she was sentenced to life in prison. She would remain behind bars until her death in November 1936.

Nellie Koulik was acquitted on all charges.

Velma Barfield

Margie Velma Bullard entered the world on October 29, 1932, the second of nine children born to Murphy Bullard and his wife, Lillie. The Murphy's were poor farmers, their homestead without electricity, plumbing or running water. These were not the only hardships for the Bullard children, though. Murphy Bullard was a strict disciplinarian, who particularly disliked backchat. As Velma was a willful child with a smart mouth, she warranted regular strap beatings.

In the fall of 1939, Velma gained some respite from the conditions at home when she started school. She was an intelligent girl, but a social outcast, mocked and picked on by the other children who made fun of her outmoded clothes and paltry lunches. She soon became isolated from her classmates. She also started stealing, pilfering coins from her father to buy candy. There were more serious indiscretions, too. She once stole $80 from an elderly neighbor, earning her a severe beating.

But despite his harsh discipline, Velma's siblings considered Velma to be Murphy Bullard's favorite. Velma would later claim that it was more than that, that her father had, in fact, sexually abused her in adolescence. However, her siblings furiously dispute these allegations and insist that Murphy never behaved inappropriately towards any of his children.

By 1946, Velma was in high school, where she was the star of the girls' basketball team. She was also in love. Thomas Burke was a lanky youth, a year older than Velma. He was a gentle soul with a good sense of humor and the two were inseparable. However, Murphy would not allow Velma to date until she turned 16, and even then, only under very strict conditions.

When Velma was 17, Thomas proposed and despite Murphy Bullard objections, the couple quit school and got married. Thomas got a job in a cotton mill while Velma looked after the home. On December 15, 1951, their son, Ronald Thomas Burke was born, and on September 3, 1953, Velma gave birth to a daughter, Kim.

Velma adored being a mother, and she was an excellent one, tolerant, conscientious and devoted. She regularly took her children to the local Baptist church and when they started school, she became "grade mother" for both their classes. She was always available to assist with class field trips and the kids loved driving with her because she was so much fun.

Around this time, Velma got a job working the nightshift in a textile plant and with the extra money the Burkes were able to move to a nicer house in Parkton. These were good years for the Burke family. Unfortunately, troubled times lay just around the corner.

In 1963, Velma began having medical problems and had to undergo a hysterectomy. She was not overly troubled by this, as she and Thomas had already decided that they only wanted two children. However, the surgery resulted in Velma suffering from lower back pain making her often short-tempered with her husband and children. She also began suffering depression as she felt that her inability to bear children made her less of a woman.

To make matters worse, Thomas had recently joined the Jaycees, and Velma resented the time he spent away from her and the kids. She also took issue with his drinking, even if it was only an occasional few beers with his friends.
Velma was a staunch teetotaler who agreed with the teachings of her church, that alcohol was evil.

In 1965, Thomas was involved in a car accident. He claimed that he hadn't been drinking but Velma wasn't buying it and their battles over booze escalated. Soon, there were furious arguments, daily shouting matches that frightened the children and put a severe strain on the marriage.

Then things got even worse. In 1967, Thomas was arrested for drunk driving, resulting in the loss of his driver's license and, with it, his job as a truck driver at Pepsi-Cola. He was devastated and sought solace in the bottle, further exacerbating the problems in the marriage. By the time he got another job, as a mill hand, he and Velma were all but estranged.

And the tensions were taking their toll on Velma, too. One day, her son Ronnie came home to find his mother lying on the kitchen floor. He rushed her to the hospital where she remained under care for a week. She was eventually discharged with a prescription for a mild tranquilizer, Librium. Soon, she was popping Librium recreationally and looking for stronger drugs, like the Valium that was prescribed for her by another physician.

So began Velma's descent into addiction. She began visiting several doctors, obtaining prescriptions from each, mixing drugs that should never be taken together. Much of the time she existed in a haze, staggering around as unsteady as a drunk.

One day in April, while the kids were at school, and Velma was at a laundromat, the Burke's house caught on fire. The only person home at the time was Thomas Burke and although firefighters managed to pull him from the blaze, he died later from smoke inhalation. Velma collapsed when told of her husband's death.

Not long after Thomas' death, Velma began dating again. Her new beau was a widower named Jennings Barfield, who suffered from various health problems including diabetes, emphysema, and heart disease. They were married on August 23, 1970 and Velma moved into the small Fayetteville home that Jennings shared with his teenaged daughter, Nancy.

But it didn't take long before the marriage was in trouble, mainly due to Velma's addiction to prescription drugs. Twice she was rushed to hospital after overdosing and despite her promises to cut down, she showed little inclination to do so. Jennings confided to friends that the marriage had been a mistake and spoke of seeking a divorce, but he never got the chance. Jennings Barfield died of apparent heart failure on March 21, 1971.

Widowed for a second time, Velma consoled herself in her medications, upping the dosage each time a new crisis arose. And there were a few of those. First, Ronnie was drafted into the army, then Velma was fired from her job at Belk's department store, then her father died of lung cancer and finally her house burnt down again. Neither was that the end of her troubles. Ronnie's announcement

that he planned to marry sent her into deep depression. She simply
couldn't stand to share her beloved son with another woman.

In March 1972, Velma Barfield had her first run-in with the law when
she was arrested for forging a prescription. She pled guilty in April
and got off with a fine and a suspended sentence.

Meanwhile, Velma's relationship with her mother was deteriorating.
The pair quarreled constantly with Velma claiming that Lillie was
always ordering her about. Lillie, for her part, objected to Velma's pill
popping, and wasn't afraid to let her daughter know it.

During the summer of 1974, Lillie became dreadfully ill, her stomach
racked by cramps as she suffered violent bouts of vomiting and
diarrhea. It got so bad that she had to be hospitalized, but she
recovered sufficiently within a few days to be discharged. The doctors
never did find out the reason for the sudden illness but Lillie
appeared to be fine right up until Christmas.

Over the holidays, the entire Bullard clan gathered at Lillie's house. It
was a joyous time with a delicious meal and the companionship of
family. However, Lillie did raise a concern with one of her sons. She
said that she'd received a letter from a finance company threatening
repossession of her car. Except, Lillie owned the car free and clear,

she'd paid it off some time ago. The son told her it was probably a mistake and that she shouldn't worry about it.

A couple of days later, Lillie was violently ill again, the symptoms of her previous illness back with a vengeance. She was vomiting and suffered a terrible bout of diarrhea. She complained about agonizing pains in her stomach and lower back and said it felt like her insides were burning up. Eventually, when she began throwing up blood, Velma called for an ambulance. But it was too late. Within hours of arriving at the hospital, Lillie Bullard was dead.

Just weeks after Lillie's death, Velma was in trouble with the law again, this time for writing bad checks. It earned her a six-month prison term of which she served three before being released. Soon after, she began offering her services as a caregiver for the elderly.

Velma's first assignment was with Montgomery and Dollie Edwards. Montgomery, 94, was a diabetic who had lost his eyesight and both his legs to the disease. He was bedridden and incontinent. Dollie, 84, was a cancer survivor who'd had a colostomy. At first, both Velma and the Edwards seemed pleased with the caregiver/employer arrangement, but there was soon tension between Velma and Dollie. It was a surprise therefore that Dollie kept Velma on after Montgomery's death in January 1977.

On February 26, Dollie became sick with vomiting and diarrhea. When her son came to visit, he was shocked to see how pale and weak she looked. He called an ambulance to transfer Dollie to the hospital, where she died the next day.

Velma was now unemployed, although not for long. She was soon caring for 80-year-old John Henry Lee and his 76-year-old wife, Record. But it wasn't long before problems began surfacing here too. Record loved to talk and her incessant chatter got on Velma's nerves. Not only that, but Record and her husband often argued, and Velma hated being caught in the middle of their fights. Then there was the check. Record knew it had to be forged because she hadn't signed it. Yet, she had no idea who might have done such a thing. Nonetheless, John Henry insisted that the matter should be reported to the police.

A few days later, on April 27, John Henry got sick. He developed diarrhea and had to be rushed to hospital where, over the next four days, he gradually recovered. Doctors said it was likely a virus and discharged him. But throughout May, he suffered regular bouts of illness – vomiting, diarrhea, stomach cramps and cold sweats. Eventually, he had to be hospitalized again and this time there would be no recovery. The severely dehydrated, terribly sick man died on June 4.

Not long after the funeral of John Henry Lee, Velma began dating 56-year-old tobacco farmer Stuart Taylor and the couple moved in together. Taylor was a widower who enjoyed Velma's company but made it clear that he had no intention of marrying someone with a police record.

In late January 1978, Taylor and Barfield attended a revival meeting at the Cumberland County Civic Center in Fayetteville. During the service, Taylor began to complain of stomach cramps, which eventually became so bad that he had to leave the hall. After the meeting ended, Velma found him lying in the bed of his truck, writhing in agony. She took the wheel and began driving home, stopping several times along the route so that Stuart could throw up. Back at the farm, Stuart's condition continued to worsen. He complained a severe pain in his stomach, chest and arms and he vomited incessantly. He felt like he was on fire from inside, he said.

The next day, Velma drove Stuart to the hospital, where doctors examined him and diagnosed "gastritis." He was prescribed medicine and sent home that same night. Over the next few days, he seemed to recover but by the end of the week he'd taken a drastic turn for the worse. At around 8 p.m. on Friday morning, a distraught Velma phoned John McPherson, a neighbor and friend. "Stuart needs an ambulance!" she sobbed. McPherson dialed 911, then drove to the house himself. He found Taylor in an appalling condition. His complexion was chalky white, his body bathed in sweat, his arms and legs thrashing in uncoordinated movements as incoherent animalistic sounds escaped him. A stench pervaded the room as the stricken man had suffered a bout of diarrhea.

The ambulance crew worked quickly and efficiently to rush the stricken man to the hospital, but within an hour of his arrival, Stuart Taylor was dead. The doctor said he was perplexed by the death and suggested an autopsy. Taylor's adult children concurred. It was the beginning of the end for Velma Barfield.

On the day of Stuart Taylor's funeral, Lumberton Police Detective Benson Phillips got a strange phone call. The caller said that Stuart Taylor had been poisoned and that the person who had killed him was Velma Barfield. The caller also said that Velma had killed other people, including her own mother.

"How do you know about this?" Phillips asked.

"Because Velma is my sister," the caller replied.

Phillips wasn't sure what to make of the call but decided to check it out anyway. He phoned the Lumberton hospital and asked about Taylor's death. Yes, he was told, Stuart Taylor had died, but at this stage it looked like death by natural causes. They would know more once the autopsy results were in.

Meanwhile, pathologist Dr. Robert Andrews got a call from Taylor's daughter, wanting to know the outcome of the autopsy. Andrews explained that he was still waiting on test results but the woman sounded so distraught that Andrews decided to call North Carolina's chief medical examiner, Page Hudson. Hudson was not familiar with the case but asked Andrews to describe Taylor's symptoms. After listening attentively to Andrews' description, he asked a single question: "Where did she get the arsenic, Bob?"

By now, Detective Phillips, who had received the tip-off about Velma Barfield, had discovered that he did not have jurisdiction, as Stuart Taylor's home was outside the city limits. He therefore passed the details on to Sheriff Wilbur Lovett who brought Velma in for questioning. Lovett began by discussing some bad checks Velma had written, then brought the subject around to Stuart Taylor. "Do you know he was killed with arsenic?" Lovett asked. Velma seemed stunned but soon recovered her composure. She denied any complicity in Taylor's death. Without evidence to the contrary, the sheriff was forced to let her go.

The following day, Velma's son Ronnie Burke got a call from a woman claiming to be a friend of his mother. The woman told him that Velma was about to be arrested for the murder of Stuart Taylor. Ronnie drove immediately to the Lumberton Police Department and talked to Wilbur Lovett, who admitted that Velma was a suspect but refused to say more. Burke then drove to his mother's home and told her about his conversation with the sheriff. As he spoke, Velma started sobbing. "I only meant to make him sick," she wailed.

As the shocked Ronnie Burke sat and listened, his mother described how she had spiked Taylor's beer and tea with arsenic. She insisted that she hadn't meant to kill him, only to make him ill until she could pay back some money that she'd stolen from him. Relieved that it may all have been an accident, Ronnie persuaded his mother to accompany him to the police station. It was there that he'd learn the dreadful truth. His mother was not only a suspect in the murder of Stuart Taylor but in three others, including that of his maternal grandmother, Lillie Bullard.

Velma Barfield's trial for the murder of Stuart Taylor began on November 27, 1978. The prosecutor in the case was Joe Freeman Britt, a staunch advocate of the death penalty who made it clear from the start that he regarded this as a capital murder case.

Velma's lawyer, Bob Jacobson had the difficult task of trying to get the charge reduced to second-degree murder, by convincing the jury that Stuart Taylor's death had been accidental. But Velma had already confessed to the murders of Dollie Edwards, John Henry Lee, and Lillie Burke, and when the judge allowed those confessions into evidence, the outcome was a foregone conclusion. On December 2, 1978, the jury returned a guilty verdict with a recommendation of the death penalty.

The sentence was appealed of course, but as one petition after another was turned down, Velma appeared to resign herself to her fate. She began corresponding with the famed evangelist Billy Graham and recommitted her life to Christ; she started working as an unofficial counselor, helping new inmates adapt to prison life; she co-authored a book about her experiences titled "Woman on Death Row." And as her execution date approached, she came clean about two other murders, those of her husbands, Thomas Burke and Jennings Barfield.

On November 2, 1984, dressed in pink pajamas and an adult diaper, Velma went to the death chamber. As the mix of chemicals that would end her life began to flow, she was told to count backwards from 100. "One hundred, ninety-nine, ninety-eight . . ." she began before her voice started to slur. She was pronounced dead at 2:15 a.m.

Helene Jegado

The case of Helene Jegado is one of the most infamous in French criminal history. Jegado was an iterant domestic worker and enthusiastic poisoner who lived in the early years of the French republic. A truly callous woman, she was a kleptomaniac who killed to cover up her petty thefts, to settle trivial arguments, and for the sheer pleasure it appeared to give her.

Jegado was born on a farm near Lorient in Brittany, France in 1803. Orphaned at the age of seven, she was raised by two aunts who were domestic servants. When Helene was 16, one of those aunts got her a position with her employer, a priest named M. Conan. Helene had barely started her new job when a shepherdess, also employed by M. Conan, accused Helene of trying to poison her. Nothing came of the accusation. It was not until 1833, that the first death could be attributed to Helene Jegado.

In June of that year, she entered the service of another priest, one M. Le Drogo. Within three months, seven people in the household were dead, all of them succumbing to convulsions and vomiting after eating food prepared by Helene. Included among the victims was Helene's own sister, Anne, who had died while visiting Helene. Eventually, Le Drogo himself died, his death and the others attributed to a cholera outbreak that was ravaging the region at that time.

Helene moved next to Bubry, taking up the position left vacant by her sister Anne's death. And it wasn't long before three members of the household, including her employer's 16-year-old daughter, were dead. The girl had shown no sign of illness prior to Helene's arrival. Helene tended each of the victims to the last and made a great show of remorse at their passing.

We next find Helene in Locmine, where she gained employment as an apprentice to a seamstress, Marie-Jeanne Leboucher. Marie-Jeanne and one of her daughters were soon grievously ill and died within days. Her son also became ill and survived only because he refused to allow Helene to nurse him.

Out of work and with nowhere to go, Helene found shelter in the home of the widow Lorey and repaid her benefactor by feeding her arsenic-laced soup.

Thirteen people associated with Helene Jegado had died in the space of just eighteen months. But she was far from done.

In May 1835, Helene entered the service of Mme. Toussaint of Locmine. Within a month four people in the home died in agony, after eating a vegetable soup prepared by the new maid. Apparently distraught by these latest deaths, Helene then committed herself to a convent. But even here, her malicious nature was soon to the fore. Small items began to go missing and household fixtures were vandalized. Helene was eventually asked to leave.

Returning to her one-time trade as an apprentice seamstress, Helene next found work with 77-year-old Anne Lecouvrec in Auray. The old lady was dead within two days of Helene's arrival, at which Helene was heard to remark, "All I carry is sorrow. My masters die wherever I go!"

Helene traveled next to Ploermel, and then to Auray, leaving behind a poisoned woman at each location. Then she got a job as a cook with the Jouanno family in Pontivy and proceeded to murder her employer's 14-year-old son. Another employer, M. Kerallic, died after consuming a drink that Helene had prepared for him. Then, with questions beginning to be raised about the trail of destruction that seemed to follow in her wake, Helene dropped out of sight. She'd keep a low profile for the next three years, emerging in 1839, to murder Mme. Veron, a dowager who succumbed to violent vomiting while under Helene's care.

Two more years passed. In 1841, Helene was in service with the Dupuy family in Lorient, when the family's young daughter died. She'd barely been buried when other members of the family began to suffer convulsions, vomiting, and numbness in the extremities. They survived, but M. Dupuy and his older daughter would be afflicted with partial paralysis for years after.

By now, Helene Jegado had acquired an unsavory reputation in Lorient and she departed for pastures new, dropping from sight for most of the next decade. While it is unlikely that so prolific a killer would have remained inactive for such a long period, there were no more murders during this time that can be positively attributed to her. When she reappeared, in Rennes in 1848, she seemed to have taken to drink. Her thefts from this point on were mainly of wine and brandy, pilfered from her employers. It resulted in her dismissal from several households.

In November 1849, she was working as a domestic servant to a couple named Rabot when their son, Albert, died after eating some porridge cooked by Helene. Albert's death did not raise any suspicion, but two months later M. Rabat caught Helene raiding the wine cabinet. He gave her ten days' notice. Before she departed she fed him and his wife a poisoned stew. They survived but were paralyzed for months afterwards.

There was a death at Jegado's next place of employment as well. This time, she murdered the young son of a family named Ozanne, in revenge for being scolded for stealing wine. She moved next to work for M. Roussel, proprietor of the Hotel Bout-du-Monde in Rennes. Some six weeks later, Roussel's mother had occasion to reproach Helene for her insubordinate attitude. Soon after, she became ill after eating a meal Helene had prepared. She did not die immediately but remained sickly for the rest of her life.

While working at the hotel, Helene became jealous of another maid, a woman of 30, named Perrotte Mace. In mid-August, Perrotte fell ill, with symptoms that included vomiting, pains in the stomach and limbs, distension of the abdomen, and swelling of the feet. She died on September 1, 1850, and although doctors suspected poisoning, her family refused an autopsy. A short while later Helene was dismissed after being caught red-handed, stealing wine.

Helene was not out of work for long, but her next position, with a law professor named M. Bidard, would be her last. In late 1850, one of M. Bidard's servants, Rose Tessier, became ill and died. Then in June 1851, another servant girl, Rosalie Sarrazin, began showing similar symptoms, vomiting, severe abdominal pains and numbness in the extremities. Doctors were called and fought to save Rosalie's life but to no avail.

An autopsy was ordered, but to the surprise of the physicians (who suspected poisoning) there was no trace of arsenic. Still, the two men were convinced that Rosalie had been poisoned and when they heard that another servant girl had died in similar circumstances, they decided to take their case to the Procureur-General. He, in turn, resolved to call on the home of M. Bidard personally.

The Procureur-General, along with the two doctors, arrived at the Bidard residence on July 1, 1851. They were admitted and sat down to speak with M. Bidard. However, they'd only just announced the purpose of their visit when one of the servants, standing close by, blurted out. "I am innocent!"

"Innocent of what?" the Procureur-General demanded of Helene Jegado. "No one has accused you of anything." Jegado was arrested soon after. Later inquiries would link her to at least 23 deaths between 1833 and 1851.

Helene Jegado's trial began on December 6, 1851. Due to the French law of prescription legale (a 10-year statute of limitations) she was accused of only three murders, together with three attempted murders and numerous thefts. She denied all of the charges, even declaring that she had no idea what arsenic was. It did her no good. Found guilty on all charges she was sentenced to die.

Jegado was put to death by guillotine on the Champ-de-Mars in Rennes on February 26, 1852, watched by a crowd of thousands.

Louise Peete

Louise Peete was born Lofie Louise Preslar, in Bienville, Louisiana, on September 20, 1880. The daughter of a wealthy newspaper publisher, she lacked for nothing during her childhood and was educated at the best private schools. And it was perhaps due to her gilded upbringing that she grew to be a precocious young thing, who was sexually active when she was barely into her teens. She was also of a somewhat light-fingered disposition and after being found in possession of jewelry that belonged to her classmates, she was expelled from finishing school and returned to Bienville in disgrace.

Not that it appeared to bother Louise too much. Her father's money saw to it that she didn't need to work and so she indulged herself in a life of leisure. She remained living under her parents' roof until 1903, when she met a man named Henry Bosley, a traveling salesman and sometime jazz drummer. Louise was fascinated by his tall tales of life on the road and so when he left Bienville, she went with him. By then, they were already man and wife.

Henry Bosley thought of himself as a man of the world. But he had no idea of what he was getting into. Louise might have appeared innocent and demure but she enjoyed flirting with other men and taking things that didn't belong to her. After being run out of Tulsa, Oklahoma over some jewels Louise had pilfered, the couple departed for Waco, Texas. There, Bosley returned from work one day to find his wife in bed with another man. Devastated by her betrayal, Bosley blew his own brains out two days later.

A few weeks Henry's death, Louise Bosley showed up in Boston, Massachusetts, using the name Anna Lee Gould and claiming to be a European noble who'd fallen on hard times. Soon she'd landed herself a job in one of the city's high-class whorehouses and was building up a steady clientele of Boston grandees. But, as ever, Louise just could not resist the lure of her wealthy clients' belongings. Eventually caught in the act, she was ejected from the house. She then fled west, to Dallas, Texas, where she wooed oilman Joe Appel, a flamboyant character, known for his extravagant diamond rings and diamond-studded belt buckles. One week after meeting Louise, Appel was found dead from a bullet wound to the head. Most of his jewelry was also missing.

Louise was hauled in for questioning and readily admitted shooting Appel. However, she claimed that she had acted in self-defense, after Appel had tried to rape her. When the matter came before a grand jury, Louise put up such a tearfully convincing performance in the witness box that she was acquitted, with the members of the jury actually applauding as the judge set her free. No one, it appears, thought to ask about the missing jewels.

But the ill-gotten windfall brought Louise only a short period of solace. By 1913, she was out of cash and down on her luck. When hotel clerk Harry Faurote asked for her hand in marriage, she accepted, seeing it as a way out of her predicament. Then Faroute was quickly schooled in the lessons that Henry Bosley had learned before him. Louise was not the caring, considerate woman she pretended to be. She was a man-eater with a voracious sexual appetite. Driven to despair by his wife's frequent infidelities, Faurote hung himself in the hotel basement in 1914.

Things in Dallas hadn't worked out quite as Louise had hoped. After Harry Faurote died, she moved to Denver, Colorado, where she'd soon hooked Richard C. Peete, the owner of a Hudson automobile franchise. She married him in 1915 and bore him a daughter a year later.

As far as Louise Peete's multiple marriages went, this one was relatively stable. That is to say, she stuck it out for five years before boredom got the better of her. Louise was just not cut out for the life of a housewife and mother. In 1920, Richard arrived home one day to find that Louise had abandoned him and their daughter. She'd taken off for Los Angeles where she hoped to find a man who could keep her in the manner she expected. The man she decided on was mining executive, Jacob Denton. After securing a job as a housekeeper to the wealthy widower, she got immediately to work on seducing him.

Denton, like just about every man Louise encountered, was soon under her spell. By now in her late thirties, she was still an attractive woman and one who was exceptionally talented in the bedroom. But sex was one thing and marriage quite another. Although Louise pressed him to "make an honest woman of her" Denton refused. That was a mistake. On May 30, 1920, Denton disappeared and Louise took over his 14-room mansion on South Catalina Street. She told contradictory stories about his whereabouts, some of them quite ludicrous. First, she claimed that he had run off with "some Spanish woman." Then she said that he'd gone to Portland on business, then to Arizona. Finally, she claimed that he'd had to have his arm amputated due to an infection and was so embarrassed by his deformity that he'd gone into hiding.

For two months, Louise managed to keep Denton's family at bay with her ever evolving stories. In the interim, she threw a series of lavish parties at the Denton mansion, an ill-advised move that saw the family hire an attorney to get to the bottom of things. He in turn, employed a private investigator, A.J. Cody, who showed up at the mansion asking awkward questions. Shortly thereafter, Louise Peete quit town, fleeing to Colorado, where she hoped for a reconciliation with her estranged husband. That gave Cody the opportunity to properly search the house, something that Louise had previously blocked. Jacob Denton's decomposed corpse was found in the basement of his home on September 23, 1920. His hands and feet were bound and a .38 bullet was lodged in his brain.

It did not take the police long to track the missing "Mrs. Denton" to Denver, where Richard Peete had welcomed her back with open arms. She was extradited to California to stand trial for murder. Convicted on that charge in January 1921, she was sentenced to life in prison.

The Louise Peete story might have ended right there, with the protagonist behind bars for the rest of her days. But there are still a number of twists to this convoluted tale. First, there was the death of Richard Peete, the cuckolded husband who continued to believe in his wife's innocence even when all of the evidence screamed "Guilty!" Peete continued to write to Louise while she was in prison but in 1924, she suddenly stopped answering his letters. When all entreaties on his part failed to get a response, Peete became the third of Louise's husbands to take his own life, hanging himself in a seedy Tucson hotel room.

According to, Clinton Duffy, warden of San Quentin, Louise liked to boast about the men who had killed themselves on her account. But she particularly cherished Richard Peete's suicide, bragging that "not even prison walls could contain her charms."

In 1939, at the tenth time of asking, Louise Peete was finally paroled, having served 18 years of her life term. After her release, she found work at a serviceman's canteen and befriended an elderly co-worker. Within months, the woman disappeared, with a police search revealing that her home had been ransacked. Louise was questioned about the disappearance, but the police apparently did no checks into her background and the matter went no further.

Then, in May 1944, Louise married for a fourth time, tying the knot with an elderly bank manager named Lee Judson. Shortly after, Margaret Logan, a woman who had worked tirelessly to secure Peete's parole, vanished. Louise was working for the Logans at the time, caring for Margaret's elderly husband, Arthur. When Arthur asked about his wife's whereabouts, Louise told him that she was in the hospital and was not allowed to receive visitors. In the interim, she was petitioning the authorities to commit Arthur to a mental hospital, a move that eventually succeeded. When he died six months later, Louise took possession of the Logan house and moved in with her husband.

Over the months that followed, Louise continued to submit reports to her parole officer, ostensibly from Margaret Logan. But by December 1944, the parole officer had become suspicious. The glowing reports did not appear to be in Mrs. Logan's hand and the signatures looked particularly dubious. Eventually, he alerted the police and they carried out a raid on the home. There, buried in the garden, they found Margaret Logan's body, a bullet in her back and her skull caved in by a heavy object.

Louise was charged with murder, her husband booked as an accessory, although he'd later be acquitted. The day after his release, on January 12, 1945, Lee Judson threw himself from the 13th floor of a Los Angeles office tower, becoming the fourth man to commit suicide on account of Louise Peete. Six months later, on June 1, 1945, a Los Angeles jury deliberated for just three hours before finding Louise guilty of first-degree murder. She was sentenced to death.

Louise Peete was executed in the gas chamber at San Quentin on April 11, 1947. She is said to have gone calmly to her death, protesting her innocence to the end. She always had been a liar.

Anjette Lyles

Anjette Donovan Lyles was born in Macon, Georgia, on August 23, 1925. Her parents Jetta and William Donovan owned a fresh produce business and were reasonably well-off. They were also besotted with their daughter and Anjette lacked for nothing during her childhood. She grew to be a pretty, blonde girl with a friendly, outgoing personality that was offset by a steely determination to succeed at whatever she did. Not exactly blessed academically, she was nonetheless voted 'most likely to succeed' by her high school classmates. Not everyone held her in such high esteem, however. Those of a less charitable disposition called her manipulative. And although that was perhaps a harsh judgment, Anjette did seem to possess an uncanny ability to bend people to her will.

Fast forward to 1947 and Anjette had blossomed into an attractive young woman of 22, one who caught the eye of many potential suitors. Anjette, however, was determined to marry well and the man she decided on was Ben Lyles, owner of Lyles Restaurant in downtown Macon. Ben had inherited the popular eatery from his late father and was operating it with his mother Julia at the time that he and Anjette started courting. The couple married in October 1947 and their union would be blessed with two daughters, Marcia, born 1948, and Carla born in 1951. By then Anjette was already the star attraction at Lyles with a natural aptitude for the hospitality business that made her a big hit with customers.

Lyles Restaurant had been a popular venue before Anjette came on board but with her running the front-of-house it quickly became the premier eatery in Macon. But while turnover was booming, the profitability of the business was heading in the opposite direction. And it was all down to Ben Lyles. Anjette's husband was a heavy drinker with a gambling addiction and a liking for paid female companionship. Anjette could tolerate all of that. What she couldn't accept was his hands in the till, drinking and gambling away all of the restaurant's profits. The couple fought constantly over money and matters eventually came to a head when Lyles announced that he was selling the business at a knockdown $2,500 in order to settle his gambling debts.

Anjette was heartbroken by the sale of the restaurant. However, the determination that was so ingrained in her personality remained intact. She resolved there and then that she'd one day buy the business back and restore it to its former glory. That she realized was never going to happen while she remained shackled to a loser like Ben Lyles.

In December 1951, six months after the sale of the restaurant, Ben Lyles was suddenly afflicted with a mysterious illness. The ailment manifested in bizarre ways. He began bleeding profusely from his nose and mouth; his legs and arms swelled; his body at times became extremely rigid as a board while at other times his limbs twitched convulsively. At times he was in such pain that he begged Anjette to shoot him. Eventually he lapsed into a coma and was moved to Macon Hospital. He died there on January 25, 1952, his death attributed to encephalitis.

Anjette Lyles was now 26 years old with two young children to support and no means of earning a living. Reluctantly she turned to her family for help but to a proud woman like Anjette, that cut deeply and she seldom told her parents how deep in the hole she really was. Ben had not only left her without support, he'd left her with a pile of debt. Not that Anjette was the type of person to mope and complain about her situation. Determined as always, she began looking for a job and eventually charmed the owner of the Bell House Restaurant into hiring her as a bookkeeper. Anjette, of course, had no qualification in this field but she was a quick learner and she had a wealth of knowledge about the restaurant trade. She was soon an invaluable member of staff.

But Anjette had no intention of spending her life tending to someone else's business. She was still determined to buy back Lyles and from the very first paycheck she received from the Bell House, she began putting money aside to realize her dream. Over the next three years she scrimped and saved, forgoing all pleasures and spending only on essentials. Lyle's Restaurant had in the interim fallen a long way from its lofty perch as Macon's most popular eatery, so when Anjette approached the owners in April 1955 with an offer of $12,000, they immediately accepted. A short while later the restaurant reopened as Anjette's.

Anjette's Restaurant was a hit from the start. The traditional Southern cuisine it served was good, although not spectacular. The key to its success lay in the sparkling personality of its proprietress. Anjette greeted her customers at the door with a hug and took the time to stop at each table for a chat. Her good looks and flirtatious manner made the venue particularly popular with Macon's leading male citizens, including judges, lawyers, businessmen and civic leaders. Local gossip linked Anjette romantically with several of these prominent men, but there was nothing to substantiate the rumors.

Anjette, in fact, had begun dating Joe Neal "Buddy" Gabbert, a commercial airline pilot and military veteran. In June 1955, the couple went for a short vacation to Carlsbad, New Mexico, and surprised friends and family by announcing on their return that they had married.

Wedded bliss though, would be of short duration. Four months into the marriage Buddy developed a severe rash which covered his face, chest, arms and legs. His legs and arms also swelled acutely, causing such pain that he begged to be allowed to die. Eventually his illness became so severe that he was taken to hospital. There his condition stabilized enough for him to be discharged. The respite, however, was brief. Buddy's symptoms soon returned, now supplemented by debilitating stomach pains and bouts of painful vomiting. Admitted to the VA Hospital in Dublin, Georgia, Buddy held on until December 2, when he died of kidney failure.

The doctors who had attended Buddy wanted to perform an autopsy but Anjette stoutly refused. "I promised him I'd never let anyone cut him up," she insisted. The doctors carried out the autopsy anyway but found nothing untoward.

In the wake of Buddy's death, Anjette hardly behaved like a grieving widow. She cashed in his life insurance policy, treated herself to a new Cadillac and was soon dating another pilot, Bob

Franks. She also bought a house in the suburbs and invited her former mother-in-law Julia Lyles to live with her. This had less to do with charity than Anjette's knowledge that Julia had nearly $100,000 in savings. Julia had barely moved in before Anjette was pressuring her into making a will.

In August 1957, Julia took ill. She was listless and pale and despite the heat of a Georgia summer, complained of feeling cold. As her condition worsened she began vomiting blood and her limbs swelled up and took on an unearthly purple hue. Eventually she became so ill that she was admitted to hospital. There Anjette continued to visit, bringing Julia's favorite foods from the restaurant and earning admiration from all quarters for her devotion. Meanwhile, Julia's condition continued to deteriorate and Anjette tearfully confided in acquaintances that her 'beloved mother-in-law' wasn't going to make it.

In late September, Anjette showed friends a note, ostensibly from Julia asking her to make funeral arrangements. Two days later, on September 29, Julia Lyles was dead. One-third of her estate went to her son Joseph, one-third to Anjette and the final portion to Anjette's daughters Marcia and Carla. As Anjette was named in the will as trustee for the girls, she had effectively gained $66,000 from Julia's death.

Three people who were closely associated with Anjette Lyles had now died of similarly inexplicable symptoms. And yet despite profiting handsomely from two of the deaths, no suspicion had attached to Anjette. If you had asked Anjette to explain this, she'd likely have offered a simple explanation - voodoo. Anjette had always been a deeply superstitious woman and at some point in her life she became involved in the occult. She consulted regularly with fortune tellers and witchdoctors and even tried to cast her own spells. Her restaurant staff would often find her burning candles of various colors in the kitchen and speaking to the flames. When asked, she readily explained her activities. "If you desire a certain result, you write it on a note and place it under a lit candle," she said. "You tell it what you want it to do."

But Anjette's voodoo spells appeared powerless to stop those around her coming to harm. In March 1958, her older daughter, 9-year-old Marcia, developed a bad cough. When Marcia's temperature suddenly rocketed to 106 degrees, her doctor ordered her hospitalized. Anjette, as was her wont, began immediately predicting her daughter's death. That prediction, as always, proved accurate. Despite round-the-clock medical care, Marcia's health deteriorated rapidly. She became delirious and started screaming about bugs and snakes crawling on her skin. She died in agony on April 4, 1958.

Marcia was buried in the family plot at Coleman Chapel near Wadley in eastern Georgia. At the funeral, a tearful Anjette placed a Bible and a bride doll in the little girl's coffin and then made an ominous remark to fellow mourners, "Carla says she wants to go to heaven to be with Marcia."

But Anjette's days as a serial killer were rapidly drawing to a close. While Marcia was ill in hospital, Julia Lyles' sister, Nora Bagley, had received an anonymous note suggesting that the little girl had been poisoned. Now she passed that note on to the authorities and Bibb County Coroner Lester Chapman ordered an autopsy. When tissue samples showed traces of arsenic, further disinterment's were ordered on the bodies of Ben Lyles, Julia Lyles and Buddy Gabbert. These too showed evidence of arsenic poisoning.

Anjette Lyles was brought in for questioning but stoutly denied any involvement in the deaths. In fact, she was able to provide ready explanations for at least three of them. She claimed that she had found Marcia playing with ant poison shortly before she became ill and believed that her daughter might have ingested the poison in that way. She also produced a note which she claimed was from Julia Lyles. In it, Julia confessed to killing her son and said that her own death had been suicide.

The Bibb County Sheriff was not duped by this feeble attempt at blame shifting. A cursory examination of the note by a handwriting expert quickly confirmed what he already suspected. Anjette may have tried to disguise the handwriting but it was obvious that she'd written the note herself.

On May 6, 1958, Anjette Lyles was arraigned for the murders of Ben Lyles, Buddy Gabbert, Julia Lyles and her daughter Marcia. She would eventually stand trial for only one murder, that of Marcia. The prosecution was, however, allowed to present evidence of the other three deaths in order to illustrate a pattern. Although mostly circumstantial, that evidence made a compelling argument for Anjette Lyle's guilt.

Witnesses testified that Anjette often screamed and swore at her daughter and had on more than one occasion threatened to kill her. Other witnesses had seen Anjette furtively pouring the contents of a bottle into drinks she intended taking to her mother-in-law and daughter at the hospital. A restaurant employee claimed to have examined the contents of the bottle and found it to be ant poison.

Hospital staff said that Anjette's behavior towards her daughter was very odd. While Marcia was suffering hallucinations and screaming about bugs on her skin, Anjette made no effort to comfort the child. Instead she stood in the corner giggling. On the day (two weeks before her death) that doctors informed Anjette that they expected Marcia to make a full recovery, Anjette went out and ordered a coffin for the girl. The following day she packed up her daughter's belongings and threw away all the flowers that had been brought for her. However, she kept the vases, saying she was going to use them at the funeral.

Other witnesses spoke of flippant remarks made by Anjette as her victims lay dying. In each case, she confidently predicted that the victim would soon be dead.

There was only one witness for the defense, Anjette Lyles herself. She read out a lengthy statement in which she vehemently denied killing her daughter or anyone else. But her icy demeanor during the trial did nothing to help her case. While complete strangers openly wept in the courtroom as details of Marcia's horrific and painful death were revealed, Anjette remained stone-faced and unmoved. It took the jury just an hour and a half to find her guilty. The judge then pronounced sentence of death.

But Anjette Lyles did not die in the electric chair. The state of Georgia had little appetite for executing a white woman, no matter how horrific her crimes. At the same time, they were acutely aware that a commutation of sentence would likely cause a public backlash. The Georgia Supreme Court therefore upheld the death sentence but ordered that Anjette be examined by a panel of medical professionals, including four psychiatrists. These experts declared her to be a paranoid schizophrenic who experienced hallucinations and claimed that she saw angels flying around the room.

Anjette Lyles' death sentence was therefore commuted and she was committed to the state mental hospital in Milledgeville, remaining there until her death of a heart attack on December 4, 1977, at the age of 52. In a bizarre end to this unusual case, Lyles was laid to rest beside her husband Ben and daughter Marcia, who she had so callously murdered.

Rhonda Bell Martin

Ronald Martin was desperately ill, struck down by an illness that had come out of nowhere and left him with debilitating cramps, numbness in his hands and feet, and bouts of diarrhea and vomiting. Attending him at his bedside, was his wife Rhonda, 20 years his senior and the light of his life. Those who knew the couple couldn't quite fathom what it was that Ron saw in Rhonda. She was certainly no looker, heavy set and bespectacled with coarse dark hair. And there was something else that was strange about Ron and Rhonda's marriage. Rhonda had previously been married to Ron's dad, Claude C. Martin. Incidentally, Claude had died just eight months earlier, of symptoms that closely mirrored those Ron was suffering now. It appeared to all concerned that he would soon be joining his father in an early grave.

And Ron Martin would almost certainly have died had friends and family not prevailed upon his wife to get him medical attention.

Rhonda, reluctant at first, eventually gave in and allowed someone to call an ambulance. It arrived not a moment too soon. The 29-year-old was rushed to a hospital in Montgomery, Alabama where doctors fought desperately to save his life. Eventually, they succeeded although Ron's survival would come at a dreadful cost. He was paralyzed from the waist down and would be confined for the rest of his life to a wheelchair. What was even more shocking was the cause of his mystery ailments. Ron Martin had been fed enough arsenic to kill a horse.

So who had dosed Ron with the deadly poison? The obvious suspect was his stout, 49-year-old wife. Rhonda was therefore brought in for questioning and it didn't take long before she was spilling the beans. Yes, she said, she had given arsenic to Ron with the intention of killing him. She'd also poisoned Ron's father (and her former husband) Claude Martin, as well as her second husband, George Garrett, her daughters, Emogene, Anna, and Ellyn, and her mother Mary Francis Gibbon.

While stunned officers tried to absorb this frankly delivered admission to wholesale slaughter, Rhonda sat impassively with her hands folded neatly in her lap. It was only when one of the investigators asked why she'd done it that she showed any emotion. "I've been trying to figure that out myself," she said in a breaking voice. "I guess I just like the funerals and the sympathy cards."

Rhonda Bell Martin was booked at first only for the attempted murder of her husband Ronald. The police had first to verify her murder confessions before taking action on those and right now they were not at all certain that Rhonda Martin was dealing from a full deck. Still, once they started delving, they quickly began putting together substantive evidence for her claims.

First, Claude Martin was exhumed and an autopsy revealed that his internal organs were riddled with arsenic. Then, investigators began looking into Rhonda's background and found that she'd been married for the first time at age 15, to a man named W.R. Alderman. That marriage had ended four years later over allegations of infidelity and spousal abuse and Alderman had walked away as the only man to wed Rhonda Martin and leave the marriage unscathed.

In 1928, Rhonda had married again, exchanging vows with George Garrett and bearing him five daughters between 1930 and 1934. All of those children would die in childhood with Rhonda admitting to poisoning Emogene, 3, Anna, 6, and Ellyn, 11. Strangely though, she refused to admit to murdering nine-year-old Elizabeth and 1-year-old Judith, even though the little girls had died of remarkably similar symptoms to their sisters.

George Garrett, meanwhile, had passed in 1939, in circumstances that mirrored the near-death of Ron Martin. The police also learned that Garrett had been insured and they now wondered if that might have been Rhonda's real motive. Sure enough, they found that Rhonda had insured the lives of each of her daughters and also of her mother, Mary Frances Gibbon. The amounts, however, were paltry, barely enough to cover the funeral expenses and certainly not a financial inducement to murder.

The motive behind the killing of Claude C. Martin was perhaps easier to unravel. Rhonda had wed Martin in 1950, eleven years after the death of George Garrett. However, she'd quickly become infatuated with her stepson, Ron Martin, and had turned to her vial of arsenic to rid herself of the impediment in her way. Within a year of wedding Rhonda, Claude Martin was dead and the widow then created a scandal by taking up with Ronald. Why she'd then decided to murder her young beau was something the police had not yet been able to figure out.

Rhonda Bell Martin was brought to trial in May 1956. In keeping with the legal protocol of the day, she was charged with just one murder, that of Claude C. Martin. This was so that the prosecution would have other cases to fall back on, should she be acquitted.

But acquittal seemed a forlorn hope for the accused. She'd already admitted to putting rat poison into her husband's food and coffee. Her lawyers therefore took the only path open to them – they pled Rhonda Martin not guilty by reason of insanity. That, in 1950's Alabama, was never likely to succeed.

On June 5, 1956, the jury deliberated for just over three hours before returning with a guilty verdict. The judge then sentenced Rhonda to die in the electric chair. On hearing the sentence, the serial poisoner put her face in her hands and sobbed bitterly.

Rhonda Bell Martin went to her death at a few minutes after midnight on October 11, 1957. After being taken from her cell to the execution chamber, she was strapped into the chair. She was then asked if she had anything to say but shook her head silently. The switch was then thrown, passing 2,200 volts of electricity through her body. Clutching her Bible in her left hand, Rhonda stiffened briefly, then went slack. A short while later she was pronounced dead, the last woman to be executed by the state of Alabama.

In the lead up to her execution, Martin had bequeathed her body to medical science, leaving a note that read:

"I want my body to be given to some scientific institution to be used as they see fit, but especially to see if someone can find out why I committed the crimes I have committed. I can't understand it, for I had no reason whatsoever. There is definitely something wrong. Can't someone find it and save someone else the agony I have been through."

In fact, the disorder that Rhonda Martin probably suffered from had already been diagnosed five years before her death. Munchausen Syndrome is a condition that causes sufferers to self-harm or invent ailments in order to garner sympathy. The variant that Martin was afflicted with is called Munchausen Syndrome by Proxy. In these cases, the sufferer harms those close to them, once again with the objective of gaining the sympathy of others.

Gertrude Baniszewski

It is one of the most horrendous crimes in the annals of American history, the systematic abuse, torture and eventual murder of an innocent 16-year-old, whose only crime was that she provoked the ire of the woman tasked with caring for her. And yet the horrific violence that Sylvia Likens endured only tells part of the story. What makes this crime even more appalling is that the torture was carried out by at least a dozen neighborhood children, some as young as ten.

Sylvia Likens was a pretty 16-year-old. Her family was from Boone County, to the northwest of Indianapolis, where her father, Lester, worked at various jobs to make a living. In July 1965, Sylvia's mother, Betty, was serving a jail term for shoplifting, leaving Sylvia to care for her younger sister Jenny, 13. Jenny was a shy, insecure girl who walked with a limp due to suffering polio as a child.

Lester Likens was at the time estranged from his wife. But he came
to hear of his daughters' plight and arrived in Indianapolis looking
for them. His inquiries led him to 3850 East New York Street, a
large rambling house owned by Gertrude Baniszewski and shared
with her seven children – Paula, 17, Stephanie, 15, John, 12, Marie,
11, Shirley, 10, James, 9, and Dennis, 18 months. Sylvia and Jenny
had come to be at the Baniszewski residence after being
introduced to Paula by a mutual acquaintance.

When Lester Likens arrived at the house, Gertrude Baniszewski
introduced herself as "Mrs. Wright." The two of them struck up a
conversation during which Lester mentioned that he and his wife
had reconciled and were planning on going on the road with a
traveling carnival. However, they had a problem as to who would
care for their children. The boys, Danny and Bennie, were staying
with their grandparents, but they had no one to care for Sylvia and
Jenny. A deal was struck, with Baniszewski agreeing to take in the
girls in exchange for $20 a week.

Nothing unusual occurred during the first week of Sylvia and
Jenny's stay with Gertrude Baniszewski. They went to school, hung
out with the Baniszewski children and attended church with
Gertrude on Sunday. But when Lester's first payment of $20 failed
to arrive, Baniszewski flew into a rage, screaming at the girls and

then forcing them to lie across a bed while she beat their bare
buttocks with a paddle.

A week later, Sylvia and Jenny went collecting soda bottles for
money to buy candy. When they returned home, Baniszewski
accused them of stealing. Sylvia tried to explain how they'd made
the money, but that only earned her another beating. When Lester
Likens arrived in town the following week to check on his girls,
neither of them mentioned that they'd been beaten.

Shortly after, the Baniszewski clan attended a church social.
Afterwards, the children told Gertrude that they were disgusted at
the amount of food Sylvia had eaten at the function. As
punishment for this transgression, Gertrude forced Sylvia to eat
hotdogs until she threw up. She then made the child scoop up the
vomit and eat it. On Lester's next visit, Sylvia did not mention the
incident to him.

By now, Baniszewski appears to have developed a pathological
hatred for Sylvia, fueled in part by Sylvia's frequent clashes with
Baniszewski's daughter, Paula. In August 1965, an incident
occurred that elevated the abuse to a new level. After overhearing
Sylvia remark that she'd allowed a boy to fondle her, Baniszewski
became enraged. She started hurling obscenities, calling Sylvia a
prostitute. She then began beating the girl, then kicking her when
she slumped to the floor. Later, when Sylvia tried to sit down,

Paula whipped the chair away. "You ain't fit to sit in chairs," she sneered. From then on, Sylvia was only allowed to sit in a chair if Gertrude Baniszewski gave her permission.

Around this time, Baniszewski began involving her children in the abuse of Sylvia Likens. She'd encourage them to play "games" with Sylvia. Those "games" usually involved Sylvia being beaten or pushed down the stairs. Soon she'd involve others, from outside her immediate family, in the torture.

The first of those was 15-year-old Coy Hubbard, Stephanie's boyfriend. Coy claimed that he'd overheard Sylvia telling classmates that Paula and Stephanie Baniszewski had sex with boys for money. In revenge, he went to the Baniszewski home and beat Sylvia. From then on, Gertrude Baniszewski encouraged Hubbard to beat and kick Sylvia whenever he wanted, and also to practice his judo on her.

Baniszewski next recruited Anna Sisco, a 13-year-old. Anna had been Sylvia's best friend, but Baniszewski convinced her that Sylvia had been spreading rumors, claiming that Anna's mother was a whore. She then instructed Anna to attack Sylvia. A similar ruse was used to recruit a friend of Paula, Judy Duke. Baniszewski even encouraged Sylvia's sister, Jenny, to join in the abuse. Jenny refused, whereupon Baniszewski punched her in the face until she complied.

Yet even as the level of abuse elevated, neither Jenny nor Sylvia said anything to their parents, or to their teachers at school. Others also had a hint of what was going on and did nothing. In August 1965, a family named Vermillion moved in next to Baniszewski. A few days later, they held a barbecue and invited Gertrude and her brood. Sylvia was sporting a black eye, which Baniszewski proudly told Phyllis Vermillion she had given her. Then, as if to illustrate her dominance over Sylvia, Baniszewski's instructed Paula to throw a cup of boiling water in Sylvia's face. Phyllis Vermillion and her husband, Raymond, saw this and did nothing.

Shortly after the incident at the barbecue, Sylvia came home from school and told Baniszewski that she needed a sweat suit for gym class. Baniszewski refused to pay for one and Sylvia then stole one from school. On seeing the new gym outfit, Baniszewski forced a confession from Sylvia, then beat and kicked her before burning the tips of each of her fingers with a cigarette lighter, in order to cure her "sticky fingers."

This "cure" precipitated a new form of abuse. Afterwards, everyone who smoked in the house took to putting out their lit cigarettes on Sylvia's skin.

A few days later, Sylvia again went collecting soda bottles. When she returned home with the money she'd earned, Baniszewski accused her of prostitution. She then forced Sylvia to strip naked in front of her sons and several neighborhood boys and masturbate with a soda bottle.

As a result of this latest incident, Sylvia lost control of her bladder and began wetting the bed. Baniszewski then declared that she was no longer fit to live with humans, and banished her to the basement. Locked down there without toilet facilities, Sylvia was forced to defecate and urinate on the floor. This enraged Baniszewski, who called her a "dirty girl" who needed to be cleansed. Baniszewski's method of achieving this was to tie Sylvia's wrists and ankles and then submerge the girl in a bath of scalding hot water. With Sylvia's burns still raw, she'd then rub handfuls of salt into her skin.

Baniszewski had by now added another recruit to her torture team. He was 14-year-old Ricky Hobbs, an honor student from a middle-class family, who had never been in any kind of trouble in his life. The boy appeared to be devoted to Baniszewski, which has left many commentators on the case to speculate that she took him as a lover. Whether that is true or not, Hobbs became Baniszewski's torturer-in-chief, carrying out her instructions without question.

While this was going on, the Baniszewski's children had turned Sylvia into a kind of freak show attraction. They charged neighborhood children a nickel a time to come and gawk at her, naked and living in the basement among her own waste. For an extra coin, the kids were allowed to beat Sylvia or push her down the stairs.

Sylvia was by now a living skeleton. She was rarely fed and when she was it was invariably a thin broth, which she was instructed to eat with her fingers. At around this time, Baniszewski's 12-year-old son, John began forcing her to eat her own feces. He also provided her with a bucket, instructing her to collect her urine in it, which he made her drink.

And yet, even now there was no help for Sylvia Likens. When Jenny managed to get a message to her older sister, Diana, detailing the abuse, Diana wrote it off as the wild imaginings of a child. When 12-year-old Judy Duke told her mother that she'd witnessed Sylvia being kicked and beaten, her mother said that Sylvia had probably earned her punishment. Even the clergy failed to get involved. When Baniszewski told her pastor, Roy Julian, about Sylvia, claiming that she was a prostitute, his only response was that they should pray for her.

While Baniszewski was accusing Sylvia of sleeping with men, her own daughter, Paula, was several months pregnant. Baniszewski would deny this to the bitter end, claiming that her daughter was a virgin, even after the signs of her pregnancy were obvious to everyone.

Diana Likens, meanwhile, was having second thoughts about the note Jenny had sent her. When she tried to visit Jenny and Sylvia, Baniszewski refused her access to the house and threatened to call the police. Concerned, Diana contacted social services. But Baniszewski turned the social worker who called at the house away. She said she'd thrown Sylvia out, as she wouldn't tolerate a prostitute under her roof. The social worker failed to check on the veracity of this story. She simply returned to her office and closed her file.

On October 21st, Baniszewski instructed John Jr., Coy Hubbard, and Stephanie to bring Sylvia up from the basement and tie her to a bed. She told Sylvia that if she could last the night without wetting the bed, she'd be allowed to sleep upstairs again. But of course, Sylvia, in her weakened condition, wasn't able to hold her bladder. As a punishment, Baniszewski forced her to perform a striptease for some neighborhood boys and then masturbate again with a soda bottle.

Afterwards, Sylvia was allowed to dress. Then, for no apparent reason, Baniszewski lost her temper and began accusing Sylvia of spreading lies about her daughters. "You have branded my daughters so I will brand you!" she screamed. She then forced Sylvia to strip and had Paula, Coy, and Ricky Hobbs gag her and tie her down, while Baniszewski's 10-year-old daughter, Shirley, heated a large sewing needle until it was red hot. Baniszewski and Hobbs used the needle to carve the words, "I'M A PROSTITUTE AND PROUD OF IT," across Sylvia's stomach. The cuts were deep, and the third-degree burns rendered by the needle would have left the scars impossible to remove, even with plastic surgery.

Baniszewski then taunted her victim. "What are you going to do now, Sylvia? You can't get married now. You can't undress in front of anyone. What are you going to do now?"

Sylvia was then untied and was carried back to the basement by Coy Hubbard. She was barely able to stand, but Hubbard still took the opportunity to practice some of his judo throws on her. That night, Jenny sneaked into the basement to visit her sister. "I'm going to die," Sylvia told her. "I can tell."

Shortly after Jenny left, Baniszewski inexplicably went down to the basement and brought Sylvia upstairs. She allowed her to sleep on one of the upstairs beds that night. At around noon the following day, Baniszewski woke her, took her into the bathroom and gave her a warm bath. She then dressed Sylvia and told her there was a letter she needed her to write to her parents. Baniszewski dictated the letter. It read as follows:

"Dear Mr. and Mrs. Likens,

I went with a gang of boys in the middle of the night. And they said that they would pay me if I would give them something so I got in the car and they all got what they wanted... and when they got finished they beat me up and left sores on my face and all over my body.

And they also put on my stomach, I am a prostitute and proud of it.

I have done just about everything that I could do just to make Gertie mad and cause Gertie more money than she's got. I've tore up a new mattress and peed on it. I have also cost Gertie doctor bills that she really can't pay and made Gertie a nervous wreck and all her kids."

For some reason, Baniszewski instructed Sylvia not to sign the letter.

After Sylvia finished the letter, Baniszewski called John Jr. and Jenny over and told them she wanted them to take Sylvia to a local garbage dump and leave her there to die. Sylvia overheard the conversation and tried to make a run for the front door. In her weakened state, she was easily hauled in. Baniszewski then beat her in the face with a curtain rod.

The following day, Baniszewski and Coy Hubbard arrived in the basement and beat Sylvia unconscious with a chair and a broomstick. That night, Sylvia tried to attract attention by banging a coal shovel against the concrete floor. Several neighbors would later report that they'd heard the commotion but decided not to call the police.

It was the last chance for Sylvia. The next day, October 26, Baniszewski told Stephanie and Ricky to bring Sylvia upstairs for a bath. They laid her fully clothed in the water but it was soon apparent that she wasn't breathing. Stephanie tried CPR, but it was too late. Sylvia Likens was dead.

With a dead body to deal with Baniszewski quickly sprung into action. She instructed her children to take Sylvia's body to the basement and strip it naked. She then sent Ricky Hobbs to a nearby payphone to call the police. When the officers arrived, she gave them the letter she'd forced Sylvia to write. The girl had been a prostitute she said and, as the letter proved, she'd been killed by her own customers.

However, even a cursory glance at the corpse told the officers that the death was not the result of a single incident, but of protracted abuse. Baniszewski, along with Paula, Stephanie, John, Hobbs, and Hubbard were arrested for murder. Other neighborhood children who were in the house at the time – Mike Monroe, Randy Lepper,

Judy Duke, and Anna Siscoe – were arrested for "injury to a
person," although the charges were later dropped. Murder charges
against Stephanie were also later dismissed, leaving Baniszewski,
Paula, John Jr., Hobbs, and Hubbard, to face the music.

Meanwhile, an autopsy on Sylvia Likens revealed the true extent of
the horror she'd endured. The body had over 100 cigarette burns,
various second and third-degree burns, severe bruising, and
muscle and nerve damage. In her death throes, she'd bitten
through her lips, nearly severing them. Her vaginal cavity was
nearly swollen shut due to repeated beatings, although an
examination proved that she was still a virgin, disproving
Baniszewski's accusation that she was a prostitute. The cause of
death was recorded as a hemorrhage of the brain.

Gertrude Baniszewski, John Baniszewski, Paula Baniszewski, Ricky
Hobbs, and Coy Hubbard, went on trial for murder in May 1966.
Despite the young age of some of the defendants (John
Baniszewski and Ricky Hobbs were just 13 and 14 respectively),
the prosecution stated its intention to seek the death penalty for
all involved. Paula's court time was interrupted when she was
rushed to the hospital to give birth to the child that her mother
had insisted she wasn't carrying.

On the stand, Gertrude Baniszewski stuck doggedly to her
assertion that Sylvia was a prostitute and a troublemaker who

caused constant discord in her home. In order to back up these accusations, her defense called the younger Baniszewski children to the stand. However, this strategy backfired spectacularly when eleven-year-old Marie Baniszewski, broke down under cross-examination.

Although she'd quite obviously been coached, the little girl suddenly screamed out, "God help me!" before branding her mother a liar and providing a graphic description of everything that had gone on in the house, of how her mother and siblings had tortured and killed Sylvia Likens.

Based in large part on Marie's testimony, Gertrude Baniszewski was found guilty of first-degree murder. However, the punishment was not the one the prosecution sought. She was sentenced to life imprisonment without the possibility of parole. A later trial would reduce that sentence to eighteen years to life.

Paula Baniszewski was convicted of second-degree murder but later struck a deal by pleading to voluntary manslaughter. She served three years before being paroled.

John Baniszewski, Coy Hubbard, and Ricky Hobbs were each convicted of voluntary manslaughter and sentenced to eighteen months in a juvenile detention facility. Hobbs was released at 17, and shortly thereafter suffered a nervous breakdown. He died of lung cancer at age 21.

After his release, John Baniszewki changed his name to John Blake. He later became a lay minister.

Gertrude Baniszewski was granted parole on December 4, 1985, despite a vociferous public campaign to oppose her release. She died of lung cancer in 1990.

A memorial commemorating Sylvia Likens was dedicated at Willard Park on East Washington Street, Indianapolis, on June 22, 2001. The house where she met her horrific death was demolished in 2009.

Shirley Turner

Afterward, when it was too late, when a child already lay dead, the question that everyone would ask was why? Why had this innocent toddler been released into the custody of a mother who was currently fighting extradition for murder? Why had that extradition process taken so long? Why had this so obviously unstable woman, this serial stalker, been allowed out on the streets? Why?

Shirley Jane Turner was born on January 28, 1961, in St. Anthony, Newfoundland. She was raised with three siblings in Wichita, Kansas. Her father was a US serviceman, her mother a Canadian national who, after the marriage broke down, moved her children back to Newfoundland. There Shirley excelled at school and was eventually accepted into Memorial University, where she planned on obtaining a medical degree.

By this time, Shirley was already showing signs of instability, nothing overt, just an overriding need for acceptance, a pathological fear of rejection. This applied particularly to her interactions with men. Shirley became easily attached and reacted badly to breakups. Still, during her first two years at Memorial, she was in a stable relationship. When she became pregnant, there was never any question that she would marry the baby's father. The couple tied the knot during Memorial University's 1981 winter recess. Their child, a boy, was born on July 9, 1982.

Over the year that followed, Turner's husband stayed home and raised their child while she continued her studies. In 1983 the couple moved to Labrador City where she obtained work as a science teacher. Two years later she gave birth to a daughter but by then, the marriage was already in trouble. Shirley had become involved in an extra-marital affair with a previous boyfriend. She left her husband in January of 1988 and married her lover in July the following year. March 1990 saw the birth of her third child, another daughter. That was followed a year later by the breakdown of her second marriage.

Shirley Turner had always been a driven individual and she proved it again in 1994 when she earned her undergraduate degree from Memorial University. This had been attained while raising her kids as a single mom and Shirley was justifiably proud of her achievement. Four years on and she had another success to celebrate, the award of her medical degree.

Here however, we begin to see a manifestation of the earlier Shirley, the one who made a habit of stalking and threatening any boyfriend who dared to leave her. Perhaps it was the pressure of the job but over the next four years, Turner developed a reputation at the medical facilities at which she served. She was described by her supervisors as manipulative and hostile, sometimes resorting to aggression to get her way, other times to tears and accusations of unfair treatment. She was also a compulsive liar, not averse to falsifying medical reports. Several patients refused to be treated by her after an initial encounter. As for her colleagues, they mostly avoided her for fear of provoking a confrontation.

One supervising physician said that she was the most difficult intern he'd worked with during his 21 years as a doctor. Another colleague went even further, describing her as "a manipulative, guiltless psychopath." That assessment notwithstanding, Turner completed the requirements of her residency. By the summer of 2000, she was qualified to practice medicine.

Shirley Turner's colleagues might have had their concerns about unleashing her, armed with a medical license, on an unsuspecting world. But in truth, they were only seeing a small part of the picture. Had they been privy to Dr. Turner's full history they'd have been positively terrified.

In March 1996, Turner began a relationship with a St. John's resident, nine years her junior. After the man called off the relationship she started stalking him, her behavior becoming so disturbing that he was eventually forced to resign from his job and leave the area. But still Turner wouldn't quit. She tracked the man to Halifax, Nova Scotia where she attacked him with a high-heeled shoe, injuring his jaw in the process. After this confrontation the man fled again, this time to Pennsylvania.

But even here he wasn't safe. Turner tracked him down and began inundating him with phone calls. Then she started showing up unannounced on his doorstep, causing such a ruckus that the police were called on several occasions to remove her. On April 7, 1999, Turner's ex-boyfriend found her lying semi-conscious outside his apartment. She was wearing a black dress and clutching a bouquet of red roses, and it turned out that she had ingested over 65 milligrams of an over-the-counter medication. Two suicide notes were found on her person. One of them read: "I am not evil, just sick."

Andrew Bagby probably knew nothing of Shirley Turner's history when he started dating her in the first half of 1999. The native of Sunnyvale, California, was studying at Memorial University when

he met Turner. The following year Turner took a job in Iowa while
Bagby stayed on at Memorial to complete his degree. After
graduating in May 2000 he landed a surgical residency in
Syracuse, New York.

During all of this time, the couple had maintained a long-distance
relationship, but the strains of such an arrangement inevitably saw
them drift apart. After Bagby took up a new position in Latrobe,
Pennsylvania, and began seeing a new woman, Turner fell into her
usual pattern and started harassing him over the phone. Matters
eventually came to a head in November 2001 when Turner visited
Latrobe and Bagby told her that it was over. She flew back to Iowa
simmering with barely suppressed rage.

Turner's plane had barely touched down in Des Moines when she
was on the phone to Bagby. His response was not what she wanted
to hear. He told her that it was over and suggested that she move
on with her life. That, in retrospect, was probably a mistake.
Shirley Turner was not a woman who dealt well with rejection.

On November 4, 2001, Turner got into her car and drove the 946
miles to Latrobe. Early the following morning she confronted
Bagby outside his residence as he was on his way to work. After
arriving at his practice, Bagby told one of his co-workers about the
incident and said that he had agreed to meet Turner later, to end
things "once and for all." The colleague begged him to reconsider,

saying that Turner "sounded dangerous." Unfortunately, Andrew
Bagby did not heed that advice. His body was found the following
morning in a parking lot at Keystone State Park. He had been shot
five times, sustaining bullet wounds to the face, chest and buttocks
before his killer finished him off with a shot to the back of the
head.

The obvious suspect was Shirley Turner but when the police
phoned her back in Iowa, she claimed that she had never left the
state and had been sick in bed on the day of the murder. That
statement turned out to be a lie, as cellphone and Internet records
detailed her cross-country journey and indicated that she had in
fact, been inside Bagby's apartment. Then there was the ballistics
report which showed that Bagby had been killed by a .22 weapon,
similar to the one registered to Turner. It was building up to be a
solid case. However, before the police could move in to arrest her,
Turner boarded a flight for Toronto.

Turner settled initially in St. John's with her oldest son. In the
meanwhile, the Pennsylvania State Police had begun extradition
proceedings and contacted the Royal Newfoundland Constabulary
with a request to place Turner under surveillance. On December
12, 2001, the same day extradition proceedings commenced
against her, the RNC moved in and took Turner into custody. Her
incarceration however, would be short-lived. Crown Prosecutor
Michael Maden released her within hours on $75,000 bail. During

her brief court appearance Turner had made an astonishing announcement. She said that she was pregnant with the child of the man she stood accused of killing.

The news that Turner was pregnant with Andrew Bagby's child added yet another twist to this already complicated case. Bagby's parents, David and Kathleen, immediately instituted proceedings to gain custody of their unborn grandchild, even relocating to Newfoundland to press their claim. After the birth of the little boy, named Zachary, in July 2002, Turner fought back. She refused to allow the Bagbys to see the child saying that she feared they would kidnap him. However, she eventually relented. When David and Kathleen attended Zachary's first birthday party, Turner appeared ready to agree to the adoption, telling Kathleen Bagby: "He obviously loves you more than me, so why don't you take him." Sadly, that would never come to pass.

In July 2003, Turner picked up a young man in a bar and the two spent the night together. The couple thereafter began dating but when Turner's new boyfriend learned of her notoriety, he broke off the relationship. A familiar pattern now followed. The man was harassed by phone and threatened with violence, eventually having to call in the police. In the meanwhile, proceedings were pressing ahead to extradite Turner to the United States, while the Bagbys were still pursuing their application for custody of Zachary. Shirley Turner's world, never on stable ground to begin with, was crashing down around her. Desperate, she decided on a way out, a sinful, selfish way that would have dreadful consequences for an innocent child.

On August 18, 2003, Turner used a prescription to obtain 30 Ativan tablets from a pharmacy in St. John's. She then drove to Conception Bay South, where her former boyfriend lived and parked her car near his house. After spiking Zachary's bottle with the anti-anxiety drug and swallowing a quantity of the tablets herself, she strapped the child to her chest in a baby carrier and jumped off a fishing pier into the ocean. Within moments they had disappeared beneath the waves.

The bodies of Shirley and Zachary Turner were recovered the following day. Both had died of drowning with the autopsy revealing that Zachary Turner had been unconscious when he entered the water and would not have suffered. That at least, was a small mercy.

The aftermath of the Turner tragedy saw a barrage of criticism directed at the Newfoundland and Labrador social services system for their failure to protect young Zachary from his obviously disturbed mother. An inquiry was launched and resulted in the passing of Zachary's Law, which would allow the courts to refuse bail if they thought that the applicant might pose a threat to his or her children. That law unfortunately came too late to save the little boy for which it was named.

Jean Lee

Marjorie Jean Maude Wright was born on December 10, 1919, in Dubbo, New South Wales, Australia, the fifth and youngest of Charles and Florence Wright's children. As a child, she attended Chatswood Public School and later a Roman Catholic convent in Sydney after her parents moved there. Jean was an intelligent girl who did well at her studies. But by high school, she was already showing the tendency towards rebelliousness that would get her into trouble in later life. She quit without graduating, thereafter drifting into a succession of low-paying jobs.

In 1938, the 18-year-old Jean was working on the production line at a canned-goods factory when she met a 25-year-old housepainter named Raymond Brees. Within months they were married and a year later, in April 1939, their daughter was born. By then the marriage was already in trouble. Brees was a work shy

individual who drank heavily and was not averse to using his fists
on his wife. Eventually, he walked out on his family and the
marriage was dissolved. Thereafter, Jean entrusted her daughter
to the care of her mother and hit the road. Her life thus far had
been one bitter disappointment after the other. It was time for her
to live a little.

But living it up required money and the only skills Jean possessed
were of the low-paying variety. She did, however, have one very
saleable asset. She was a pretty redhead with a good figure. It
wasn't long before she'd drifted into a life of prostitution,
supplementing her earnings by stealing from the American sailors
and G.I.'s that she serviced. Using the name Jean Lee, she
eventually drifted to Brisbane where she took up with a known
criminal named Morris Dias, who served as her pimp. Three years
later she dropped Dias for another lowlife, a small-time con artist
named Robert David Clayton. Then the whole cycle perpetuated
itself again. Clayton sent her out to earn her keep as a hooker
while he lived off the earnings. He also introduced her to another
way of making money, a well-worked con known as the 'Badger
game.'

The scam went something like this. Lee would work her usual
prostitution beat around Melbourne's seedy bars and hotels,
picking up men and inviting them back to her apartment for an
evening of intimate entertainment. There she'd get the mark into a

suitably compromising position before Clayton burst in, posing as her wronged husband. He would then demand a payoff in exchange for his silence. As many of the marks were married men who did not want their wives to learn of their indiscretions, most paid up and then made a hasty departure. Those who refused to pay were beaten senseless by Clayton and an accomplice named Norman Andrews. They were then robbed before being thrown out into the street. Not one of the men ever reported the assaults to the police.

The Badger game was a steady little earner for Clayton and his accomplices. But like all nickel and dime conmen, he hankered after the big score. In November 1949, he thought that he had found it. Through a criminal associate, Clayton had come to hear of William 'Pop' Kent, a wealthy recluse who owned a number of rental properties around Brisbane but made most of his income from illicit bookmaking activities. This meant of course that he could not use conventional banking channels. Hence, according to Clayton's informant, most of his money was hidden in his home.

It seemed almost too good to be true. Kent at 73 years old was unlikely to put up much resistance and would be disinclined to go to the police since that would land him in a heap of trouble over his illicit income. He was also known to have a liking for the ladies and Clayton had the perfect bait. On November 11, 1949, he sent

Lee to a hotel bar that Pop was known to frequent. It wasn't long before she'd convinced the old man to take her home.

Kent probably could not believe his luck as he escorted the attractive young redhead through the darkened streets. He would not have noticed Clayton and Andrews following at a discrete distance. By the time those two thugs burst through the door of Kent's apartment, Lee had the old man out of his clothes and was performing oral sex on him. It did not take them long to hustle Kent into a chair and bind his hands and feet. Then they got to work on him. They wanted to know where his cash was hidden and they were prepared to do just about anything to make him talk.

Kent was punched and slapped, he was stomped and tortured with a pocket knife. Yet he continued to insist that his abusers had been ill-informed, that he had no money other than his bankroll and money belt, which they had already taken. The trio then took to trashing the apartment, trying to uncover the treasure trove they had come for. Finally, they gave up and left, but not before either Clayton or Andrews strangled the old man. When the police arrived, summoned by neighbors who had heard the ruckus, they found Kent slumped in the chair. Judging by the condition of the body, he had not died an easy death.

It was a clumsy murder, committed by a trio of particularly inept criminals. Kent was well-known in the area and several witnesses had seen him in Lee's company. She, of course, had more than a passing acquaintanceship with the local constabulary, due to her history of prostitution and petty theft. She was also known to keep company with Robert Clayton and Norman Andrews. It wasn't long before the trio was tracked to their hotel and arrested, Clayton and Andrews still wearing their bloodstained clothes.

Once in custody, the gang of miscreants did what criminals do best under these circumstances – they turned on each other. Andrews was the first to crack, admitting that he'd robbed and beaten the old man but insisting that Clayton had delivered the coup de grace. Confronted with that statement Clayton made a confession of his own, in which he named Andrews as the killer. He was backed up by Lee, who admitted to robbery but denied murder. What the murderous trio did not realize was that they had just painted themselves into a corner, one that would ultimately send all of them to the gallows.

The trial of Lee, Clayton, and Andrews began at Melbourne Criminal Court on July 20, 1950, with the three defendants continuing to blame each other for Pop Kent's death. Imagine their dismay when Judge Gavan Duffy gave his instructions to the jury, outlining the concept of 'common purpose.' It did not matter which defendant had throttled Kent, the judge said, only that all three had participated in the robbery. As the murder had resulted from their decision to rob their victim, they were all equally accountable, regardless of who had actually applied the killing pressure to Kent's throat.

With those words resounding in their ears, the jury retired to consider their verdict. They were back just three hours later, having found the three defendants guilty of murder. Judge Duffy then donned the traditional 'Black Cap' and passed sentence of death. On hearing the ruling, Lee became hysterical and had to be restrained by bailiffs. Clayton and Andrews meanwhile, hurled abuse at the judge and jury.

The sentence went on appeal. And there was hope for the condemned trio when the Court of Criminal Appeal ruled with a 2-1 majority that Judge Duffy's verdict should be set aside. But the reprieve was short-lived. Prosecutors applied to the High Court to have the Appeal Court ruling nullified and they were successful in their action. Lee, Clayton, and Andrews were going to the gallows after all.

With her fate now confirmed by the courts, Jean Lee's mental health went into a steep decline. She spent hours crying and ranting and at times had to be physically restrained. She sometimes attacked her guards and on other occasions begged them to provide her with alcohol to numb her pain. There was still of course, the possibility that the State Premier would commute the sentence. Australia had not executed a woman since 1909, when Martha Rendell went to the gallows for the cruel murders of her stepchildren. Yet despite considerable public support for Lee, the Premier was unmoved.

The triple execution was scheduled for February 19, 1951, at Pentridge Prison in Brisbane. Jean Lee, as the prisoner under the greatest mental strain, was to go first, at 8 a.m. Clayton and Andrews would follow at 10 a.m., put to death in unison on the twin gallows.

Lee's execution however, did not go smoothly. As the executioners entered her cell wearing the uniquely Australian getup of goggles and felt hats, she fell into a dead faint. She was still in that condition when the hangmen pinioned her hands and feet and sat her in a chair. She was sent through the trapdoor still seated, having never regained consciousness.

Clayton and Andrews followed at 10 a.m. and appeared resigned to their fates. "Goodbye, Norman," Clayton said, just before the trap was sprung. "Goodbye, Robert," Andrews replied.

Jean Lee was the last woman executed in Australia and her death went a long way towards undermining public support for capital punishment in the country. There were other executions after hers, but only of men, the last being Ronald Ryan in 1967. Australia removed the death penalty from its statute books in 1985.

Louise Vermilyea

When Chicago police officer, Arthur Bissonette, died suddenly on October 26, 1911, his family was not only saddened, they were shocked. So too were his colleagues at the precinct where he worked. The 26-year-old patrolman had been a burly, robust fellow who until recently had been in perfect health. True, he had over the previous few days been complaining of stomach cramps and numbness in his extremities but everyone had assumed that it was just a minor bug that would soon pass. Now he was dead. Something didn't seem right and Arthur Bissonette Sr., the dead man's father, thought he knew what it was. His son had recently moved into a boarding house run by a woman named Louise Vermilyea and that move had coincided with the mysterious symptoms he had begun showing.

Bissonette Sr. didn't want to make any accusations as yet but he thought it prudent to pass on this information to his son's colleagues at the Chicago Police Department. And he had more to add too. The day after his son had moved in, Bissonette Sr. had been invited to dinner at the residence. Mrs. Vermilyea, he said, had been an immaculate hostess, fussing over her guests as they enjoyed a splendid roast. She did, however, have one rather strange custom. She gave everything on her guests' plates a liberal sprinkling with some white powder. When Bissonette asked what it was, the landlady responded that it was "white pepper." Whatever it was, it hadn't settled well with Bissonette. He had spent most of that night on the toilet bowl, hunched over with severe stomach cramps.

The story definitely seemed one worth following up and the police therefore requested an autopsy and toxicology screen on Arthur Bissonette. But even as they awaited the results they had to wonder if it was a wild goose chase. After all, Mrs. Vermilyea had hardly known Bissonette. What possible reason could she have for poisoning him? And yet, when the results came back they confirmed what Arthur's father had suspected. His son's body was riddled with arsenic. An arrest warrant was then issued for Louise Vermilyea.

The stoutly built landlady was outraged to be suspected of murder. She firmly denied any involvement in the police officer's death, making the quite reasonable observation that killing off her paying guests was hardly a sustainable business model. But as investigators started looking into the woman's background they began to pick up an alarming pattern. It appeared that people associated with Louise Vermilyea had a habit of dropping dead for no discernable reason.

The first suspicious death occurred in 1893, when Fred Brinkamp, Louise Vermilyea's first husband, passed away suddenly at the family farm near Barrington, Illinois. Brinkamp was sixty years old at the time, and although he'd appeared in good health, his death attracted no suspicion from his insurers who promptly paid the grieving widow a dividend of $5,000. And the insurance company would be obliged to make two more payments to Louise over the ensuing years, when her daughters Cora, 8, and Florence, 5, died of mystery ailments.

Louise accrued no dividend when another member of the Brinkamp clan, Fred's 26-year-old granddaughter Lillian, died suddenly in January 1906. However, it had been noted that Lillian had spoken up against Louise's upcoming marriage to Charles Vermilyea. Perhaps she should have kept her peace. Charles lasted just three years before Louise was putting him in the ground, pocketing $1,000 in the process. In the months leading up to his death, Charles had complained to family members that Louise had been pestering him to increase his life cover.

But the $1,000 insurance policy was not the full extent of Charles Vermilyea's estate. There was also a house in Crystal Lake and a family dispute soon broke out over it. Louise wanted to sell the property. Harry Vermilyea, Charles' son by a previous marriage,

believed it should be kept in the family. A number of heated rows
ensued but the matter remained unresolved until Harry's health took a
sudden turn for the worse. He died in an agony of stomach cramps and
diarrhea just weeks later.

The sale of the Crystal Lake property left Louise Vermilyea with a
handsome profit. And she'd soon be banking another insurance check
after her 23-year-old son Frank Brinkamp became ill and died.

Frank had, in fact, confided in his fiancé, Elizabeth Nolan, that he
believed his mother was poisoning him, and that she had also killed his
father and sisters. The young woman most probably regarded these as
the delirious deathbed rantings of a dying man but after Frank's death
she repeated the accusations to members of the extended Brinkamp
family. They did not appear overly surprised, suggesting perhaps that
they harbored similar suspicions. Nonetheless, no one thought to take
the matter to the authorities. Louise, in any case, had moved on to new
targets. With typical criminal cunning, she'd perceived that further
deaths in the family might prove a tipping point. Now she diverted her
attention towards the tenants at her boarding house.

On January 15, 1911, Jason Rupert, a railroad fireman, became ill after
dining with Louise. He died two days later. Just three months later,
another boarder, Richard Smith, took a turn for the worse and
subsequently died. He too had eaten a meal that had been liberally
sprinkled with Louise Vermilyea's "white pepper." And then there was

Arthur Bissonette. Vermilyea had been reckless in targeting a police officer and it had brought about her downfall.

Still the police had to wonder. What was the motive for the Rupert, Smith and Bissonette murders? The landlady had derived no material benefit from their deaths. Why then had she killed them? The answer came from a local mortician, E.N. Blocks. According to Blocks, the widow Vermilyea was obsessed with death. She would often show up at his business and offer to help prepare bodies for burial, asking no payment in return. She also appeared to have the inside track on any deaths that occurred in the neighborhood. Oftentimes, Blocks said, he would arrive at the home of a recently deceased person to find Vermilyea waiting on the doorstep for him, offering her "charitable assistance."

Louise Vermilyea had by now been charged with the murder of Arthur Bissonette and had been released on bail, although she remained under house arrest. In the interim, exhumation orders had been granted on her other suspected victims and the medical examiner's office was preparing to carry out autopsies on the remains. Louise welcomed this move which she assured everyone would clear her name. "I am innocent of the crimes laid at my door," she insisted. "I simply have been unfortunate in having people dying around me."

Unfortunately, the veracity of the statement would never be tested in a court of law. On November 4, 1911, Louise Vermilyea collapsed at her home and was rushed to hospital where it was discovered that she had ingested a large dose of arsenic. She remained hospitalized until December 9, when she eventually died, the final victim of her deadly poisoning campaign.

Pamela Smart

Just after 10 p.m. on Tuesday, May 1, 1990, 23-year-old Pamela Smart pulled her Honda CRX to a stop in front of her condo on Misty Morning Drive in Derry, New Hampshire. Pam was late coming home that evening, having attended an after-hours meeting at her job. She got out of her vehicle and walked past her husband's Toyota pickup, then climbed the stairs to the porch. The lights were out, which was unusual. Greg usually left the foyer light on when he got home before her. Nonetheless, Pam unlocked the front door, stepped inside and turned on the lights. In the next moment, she was screaming, running from the house, banging on her neighbors' doors.

"Help! My husband!" Pam shrieked, as doors began to be thrown open. "He's hurt! He's on the floor! I don't know what's wrong with him!"

By now, at least six residents had exited their units to see what the commotion was about. One of them had called 911; another, Art Hughes, was trying to calm Pam down, trying to find out what had happened.

"My husband's on the floor," was all Pam would say.

Hughes then ran towards Pam's unit, 4E. Ignoring her warning that there might still be someone in there, he pushed open the door and looked inside. A man lay face down on the carpet. He wasn't moving. There was blood, a lot of blood.

By now, both the police and ambulance service had responded to the 911 call. But there was nothing they could do for Greg Smart. An officer from the New Hampshire Medical Examiner's office made it official at 11:19. Smart was dead, killed by a bullet to the head. The yellow tape was rolled out sealing off the crime scene. Now the investigation would begin, the case assigned to Detectives Daniel Pelletier and Barry Charewicz.

Murders were a rarity in the quiet hamlet of Derry. In the year of the Smart case, Greg Smart was the only homicide victim in the town. Even so, the investigators knew a set-up job when they saw one. The murder had been made to look like a burglary gone wrong, but that didn't tally with the evidence.

For starters, there was no sign of a break-in, so how had the burglar gained entry to the residence? Why had he even chosen this condo as a target? It made absolutely no sense to carry out a burglary in a busy complex at night, when most of the residents would be home. And why had Greg Smart been shot? There were no signs of a struggle inside the house, so why had the burglar put a gun to Greg's head and pulled the trigger? Most burglars didn't even carry guns. No, the more the detectives looked at it, the more the crime scene looked to have been staged. But why? And by whom?

In any domestic homicide, the first suspect is usually the spouse, but in this case, Pamela Smart had a watertight alibi. She'd been 35 miles away, at a school meeting in Hampton. Asked if she knew who might have wanted to hurt her husband, Pam said no. Greg was a wonderful man, loved by everyone who knew him.

Pam and Greg had met at a New Year's Eve party in 1986. They'd found that they enjoyed a mutual love of rock music and had immediately hit it off. A month later they were an item. Two years after that they were married. They appeared devoted to one another.

But the marriage was hardly a year old when it was in trouble. Pam felt that Greg was no longer the man she'd fallen in love with.

She'd been attracted by his shoulder length hair and fun-loving nature. Now he'd shorn his locks and was making a living, a good living admittedly, as an insurance salesman. Pam had fallen for a rocker. Now, it appeared, she was married to a yuppie.

Worse was to come as they approached their first wedding anniversary. Greg admitted to Pam that he'd been having an affair. It was over now, he said, and he was determined to make their marriage work. A week later, he flew Pam to Florida for an anniversary celebration. On the surface, she forgave him his indiscretion but whenever they had an argument she'd bring up his betrayal. Privately, she'd already decided. She wanted out of the marriage.

In the fall of 1989, Pamela was offered a job as media services director with the school board in Hampton, some 35 miles from Derry. Having completed a BA degree at the University of Florida in 1988, she was determined to pursue a career in broadcasting, so this wasn't exactly what she was after. Nonetheless, she believed that it might be a stepping-stone, and so she accepted. Her responsibilities included producing and distributing educational videos for the school district. She was given a full-time secretary and a student intern.

She also volunteered as a facilitator for a school drug awareness program called Project Self-Esteem, where she was soon impressing the kids with her encyclopedic knowledge of rock and heavy metal music. One of those who was definitely impressed was 15-year-old Billy Flynn. The first time he saw Pam, he announced to his friend, Vance "JR" Lattime Jr., "I'm in love."

Pam met Billy Flynn not long after Greg confessed his affair to her. Billy was tall for his age, standing 5-feet-11. He had shoulder-length hair and, like Pam, he loved rock music. He also played the guitar. He was, in other words, everything that Greg no longer was in Pam's eyes. When he began hanging around the SAU building where she worked, she did nothing to discourage him. In fact, she involved him in some of the projects she was working on.

Also around this time, Pam befriended another teenager, Cecelia Pierce, who'd been designated as her student intern. Cecelia wanted to be a journalist and was soon in awe of Pam. Despite the discrepancy in their ages, the two began spending a lot of time together, frequenting malls and restaurants and clubs. Sometimes they hung out at Pam's condo. Billy Flynn usually tagged along.

Pam first hinted to Billy about her feelings for him in February 1990. Three weeks later, they kissed for the first time, while sitting on the bed at Pam's condo. Billy, who was still a virgin, was stunned. Here was this attractive older woman, the object of his boyish fantasies, and she was kissing him, telling him how much she cared for him. Right at that moment, he would have done anything for her. He could not have imagined how soon his juvenile devotion would be put to the test.

Late in March, while Greg was out of town at a conference, Pam invited Billy and Cecelia over to her condo to watch some movies, one of which was 9 ½ Weeks, a steamy thriller starring Kim Basinger and Mickey Rourke. After the movie ended, Pam asked Cecelia to take her Shih Tzu, Halen, for a walk. While Cecelia was away, she took Billy upstairs and they had sex for the first time.

During the weeks that followed, Pam and Billy got together regularly for sex. Then Pam dropped a bombshell on young Billy's life. She told him that she was ending their relationship. She couldn't let Greg find out about them, otherwise he'd divorce her and she'd lose everything, the condo, the furniture, everything. Worst of all, Greg would take Halen away from her and she couldn't bear to be parted from her little dog. She also hinted that Greg was abusive and that he often beat her. "If you want to keep seeing me, you'll have to get rid of Greg," she told Billy.

At first, Billy was shocked at the idea, but as Pam kept pressing him, he eventually agreed that he would kill Greg. Twice he put in place advanced plans to carry out the murder but changed his mind at the last moment.

Pam was furious. "If you loved me, you'd do this!" she screamed. Billy said that he did love her. "Then you'd better get rid of Greg, or you're going to lose me," she threatened.

"That's when I started getting serious about it," Billy would later tell the jury at his trial. "Because I thought that if I did nothing, she was going to leave me and that would be it."

Not long after, Billy started talking to his friends, JR Lattime and Pete Randall, about helping him kill Greg Smart. Pam had told him that May 1 would be his last opportunity. She even threw in a sweetener, offering to pay him and his accomplices out of the insurance money she was going to collect after Greg's death.

Tuesday morning, May 1, played out like any other in the Smart household, with one key difference. Usually, Pam left the house before Greg, but this day she made some excuse to stay behind. The reason was simple. She had to leave a door unlocked so that her young assassins could gain access.

Later that afternoon, Pam spoke to Billy at his school, telling him that the door had been left open as arranged. At around 8:00 p.m., while JR and another teenager, Raymond Fowler, waited in a getaway car, Billy and Pete Randall entered the condo. Their first job was to move Halen down to the basement. Pam had given strict instructions that the dog was not to be harmed or traumatized in any way.

Billy and Pete then ransacked the house, in order to make it look like the murder had happened in the course of a botched robbery. Then the two teenagers waited in the dark for their victim to arrive. Billy had a snub-nosed .38 revolver shoved into his waistband, that JR had taken from his father's gun collection.

At around 8:30, the sweep of a car's headlights briefly illuminated the foyer before being extinguished. The vehicle's engine was cut off. Minutes later came the sound of footfalls on the porch, then a key rattling in the lock. The door swung open, Greg Smart calling out for his dog even before he'd stepped through. Then he was in the foyer and Billy, who'd been hiding behind the door, responded.

He rushed Greg from behind, pushing him to the ground. Then Pete joined the fray and between the two of them they subdued their target. Greg, thinking it was a robbery, told them to take his billfold. Billy raised the gun and held it just two inches from Greg's head. "God forgive me," he said and then pulled the trigger.

Pam Smart's demeanor after the murder surprised investigators. She seemed much too calm, hardly distressed at all. A few days after Greg's death, she asked if she could go back to her home to pick up some things. There, she walked directly through the patch of her dead husband's dried blood on the carpet, barely giving it a second glance. These scarcely seemed like the actions of a grieving widow. It wasn't long before investigators began to suspect that she might have been involved in Greg's death.

And two weeks later, they had something to hang those suspicions on. An anonymous female tipster called in to say that Pam had persuaded three teenaged boys to kill her husband and that a girl named Cecelia Pierce knew about it.

On Sunday, June 10, there was another surprise development in the case. JR's father, Vance Lattime Sr., walked into the Seabrook police station and slapped down a snub-nosed .38-caliber revolver on the counter. Lattime said that he'd overheard his son and Pete Randall discussing the murder of Greg Smart and that he believed that this might be the murder weapon.

Things began to fall apart quickly for the conspirators after that. On Monday, June 11, the police brought in Lattime and Randall, as well as Cecelia Pierce. The boys weren't talking, but Pierce eventually broke down and admitted all she knew about the murder, naming Pam Smart and Billy Flynn. The following day, Detectives Pelletier and Charewicz convinced her to help them gather evidence against Pam.

Over the weeks that followed, the police set up two taped phone calls between Cecilia and Pam and also got Cecelia to wear a wire for two meetings between the pair. During the course of those conversations, Pam implicated herself in the murders, stating confidently that, if it came down to her word against that of the boys, the police would believe her.

She was wrong about that. At around 1 p.m. on Wednesday, August 1, officers arrived at Pam Smart's office and took her into custody. The charge was first-degree murder.

Pam Smart went on trial at the Rockingham County Superior Court on March 4, 1991. She readily admitted to having an affair with Billy Flynn but denied that she'd coerced Flynn into killing her husband. According to her version of events, Flynn had become obsessed with her and had killed Greg so that he could have her for himself.

Unfortunately for Pam, the evidence, especially that gathered from her taped conversations with Cecelia Pierce, said otherwise. Found guilty of murder, she was sentenced to life in prison, without the possibility of parole. She remains behind bars to this day, still protesting her innocence.

Of the other defendants, Billy Flynn and Pete Randall each got 40 years in prison, while JR Lattime got 30 years. Lattime's sentence was later reduced and he was released on parole in 2005.

Jane Toppan

For as long as there have been medical professionals tending to the sick and ailing, there have been those who have taken advantage of their privileged positions to prey on the patients under their care. In more recent times we've read with horror about doctors like Harold Shipman and Michael Swango, nurses like Donald Harvey and the malevolent Beverley Allitt. Long before these psychopaths hit the front pages though, there were medical monsters like H.H. Holmes, Thomas Neill Cream, and William Palmer. Another of this ilk was Jane Toppan, a jovial, buxom woman whose reputation for competence earned her nursing positions with many of New England's most prominent families. Little did they know that 'Jolly Jane,' the woman to whom they'd entrusted the lives of their loved ones, was one of the most depraved killers in the annals of American crime.

Like most serial killers Jane Toppan (born Honora Kelley in Boston in 1857) had a difficult start to life. Her parents were poor Irish immigrants, her father a violent drunk who was so prone to eccentric behavior that he was given the nickname 'Kelley the Crackpot.' On one memorable occasion, he tried to sew his own eyelids together while working as a tailor. Stories of his other bizarre exploits were legend among Boston's Irish community. Still, Honora had her mother as a buffer against the harshness of the world. Bridget Kelley was by all accounts a good parent and a hard worker but she died of tuberculosis when Honora was still a child. Not long after, Kelley the Crackpot was committed to an asylum.

Alone in the world, Honora and her three sisters were sent to an orphanage, although she did not remain long under state supervision. In 1865 she was placed in the care of Mr. Abner Toppan and his wife Ann, of Lowell, Massachusetts. It wasn't an adoption as such, more a kind of indentured servitude that was common in those days. The Toppans treated Jane almost as well as they did their own children but she was never left in any doubt as to her position in the household. She was a live-in maid, expected to wait on the family members and clean up after them. Abner Toppan did however give her his family title and also changed her first name from Honora to Jane. He'd live to regret that decision. It was as Jane Toppan that Honora entered the annals of infamy.

That, however, lay in the future. For now, the newly Christened
Jane was as happy as she'd been in her short life. Hard work held
no fear for her and she seemed to easily deflect the barbs that
were directed at her. She was an exemplary maidservant and a
companion of so sunny a disposition that she earned the nickname
'Jolly Jane.' Not only that but she excelled at her schoolwork, easily
bettering the academic performance of the Toppan children.

That, at least, was the face that Jane Toppan showed to the world.
But below the surface, a sinister persona lurked. By her teens, she
was already displaying many of the behaviors of the fledgling
serial killer. She had become a habitual thief and a compulsive liar
who enjoyed spreading malicious rumors about people she
disliked. She was also an enthusiastic pyromaniac, deriving sexual
pleasure from the fires that she set.

This particular set of behaviors is almost textbook in the making of
a psychopath. They express an innate need for control, a desire to
mislead, manipulate and destroy. And it is perhaps unsurprising
that Jane chose nursing as a career. After all, medical professionals
often wield the power of life and death over their patients. To a
personality as warped as Jane Toppan, that must have been an
intoxicating prospect.

In 1885, Toppan enrolled as a student nurse at Cambridge
Hospital in Massachusetts. There she excelled at her studies,

graduating near the top of her class. Even so, there were concerns expressed by hospital administrators regarding her apparent obsession with cadavers and autopsies. Jane could often be seen attending extra anatomy classes, elbowing her way to a spot beside the autopsy table as the corpse was opened up. Her fellow students would later testify that she appeared almost to be salivating as she watched the macabre spectacle. Teachers would express their concern about the glint in her eye, the little smile that played continuously on her lips.

Still, there was nothing in the rule book that prevented a student showing interest in her studies. After graduating with honors, Jane was taken on as a trainee nurse at Cambridge. A short while later there was an upsurge in deaths at the hospital.

According to Toppan's later confession, she initially started drugging patients with morphine and atropine in order to gauge their reactions. This was no casual undertaking. Toppan took to her project like a mad scientist, conducting a whole series of sick experiments. She began by altering the prescribed dosage, first withholding medication and then overdosing the patient to see what effect it would have. Toppan was a quick study and she kept meticulous notes so it wasn't long before she'd perfected her methodology. Her aim was to inflict maximum suffering, to keep the patient hovering on the verge of death for as long as possible. This was achieved by doping the patient into unconsciousness, reviving him briefly and then rendering him unconscious again. Then as the patient took his last breaths, Toppan would climb into bed and hold him as his life slipped away. At the moment that he drew his final breath, she was so elated that she was often brought to a shuddering orgasm.

Given the euphoria that Toppan derived from the act of murder, it is unsurprising that she repeated it many times. Yet despite the high number of patients that died under Toppan's care, no suspicion seems to have accrued to her. In fact, her reputation as a competent nurse had spread beyond the walls of Cambridge and in 1889 she was offered a position at the prestigious Massachusetts General Hospital. She would remain there for just over a year, during which she barely missed a beat in continuing her killing spree. This time however, the high casualty numbers on her shift did not go unnoticed. The hospital administrators should probably have alerted the authorities but they wanted to avoid a scandal and so they hauled Jane before a disciplinary board and dismissed her for negligence.

Toppan was not out of employment for long. She was soon back at her old stomping ground and just as soon back in the business of mass slaughter. Unfortunately for Toppan, an employee at Massachusetts General had forewarned one of his colleagues in Cambridge and it wasn't long before Toppan found herself the subject of disciplinary action again, accused of the 'reckless prescription of opiates.' Toppan would spend much of the hearing giggling softly to herself, so it was not surprising when the board terminated her employment. However, they again decided not to involve the police, an absurdly reckless call given Toppan's record. Instead, they put the word out and Toppan found herself blackballed. There wasn't a hospital in New England that would employ her.

A short while later an advertisement appeared in various Massachusetts dailies, offering the services of a 'qualified and compassionate nurse, skilled at caring for the aged.' Such services were of course much in demand among those who could afford them. It wasn't long before Toppan found herself employed by a wealthy New England family. In no time at all, the woman assigned to her care had 'passed peacefully in her sleep' and Toppan was sent to a new home with the ringing endorsement of her previous employer. Sure enough, death followed here too and there was also an accusation of petty theft. Still, that seems to have done no harm to Jolly Jane's employment prospects. She was seldom out of work, even if few of her clients appeared to survive her ministrations.

Private practice though had one major drawback for Toppan. It denied her access to the steady stream of potential victims that her murderous urges demanded. The occasional domestic homicide was all very well but a murder every few months simply did not suffice. Toppan began casting around for fresh victims, starting with her landlord and his wife in 1895 and then honing in on friends and family, culminating in the murder of her foster sister Elizabeth in 1899.

In the summer of 1901, Toppan was vacationing at a cottage in Cataumet, owned by an old friend Alden Davis. Within a matter of weeks, Davis and two of his daughters were dead. Toppan then moved back to Boston and began a relationship with her late foster sister's husband. Death soon followed. The man's sister died under mysterious circumstances and then he himself became ill, with Toppan insisting on taking personal responsibility for his care. She even poisoned herself to avoid suspicion. Fortunately, the man saw through the ruse and ordered Jane to leave his house. Unfortunately, he decided not to take the matter up with the police.

Toppan had once again escaped prosecution. But her luck had just about run its course. The Davis family was suspicious of the sudden deaths of Alden and his daughters. They ordered an autopsy on the youngest girl, with the toxicology report providing conclusive evidence that she'd been poisoned with strychnine. It didn't take a genius to figure out who was responsible and on October 26, 1901, Jane Toppan was arrested and charged with murder.

Toppan had no hesitation in confessing to the charges brought against her. In fact, she seemed to derive genuine pleasure from describing her crimes. The motive she said was the "irresistible sexual impulse" she derived from holding her victims in her arms as they died. She also claimed that her ambition was "to have killed more people – helpless people – than any other man or woman who ever lived."

Placed on trial at the Barnstable County Courthouse in June 1902, Toppan was found to be "morally insane," in other words a criminal psychopath. She was committed to the Taunton Insane Hospital with the stipulation that she should never be released.

Not long after that sentence was passed, The New York Journal carried an article in which Toppan confessed to 31 murders. Most observers consider this number to be well short of the mark. Based on the years she was active and the rate at which she committed her murders, it is estimated that Toppan may have been responsible for as many as 100 deaths, making her one of the most prolific American serial killers.

Jane Toppan died at Taunton on August 17, 1938, at the age of 84.

Christine Falling

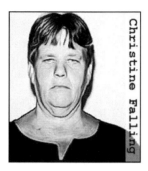

Christine Falling did not have the best start in life. Her mother, Ann, was just 16 years old when Christine entered the world on March 12, 1963. And Christine was not even her first child. Her father, on the other hand, was a violent drunk who was nearly 50 years older than his teenaged bride. At 65 years of age, Thomas Slaughter could quite easily have been his wife's grandfather. He was often unemployed. When he did work, the meager wage he earned as a laborer was barely enough to feed and house his family.

Growing up in these conditions could not have been easy for Christine. But life had also dealt her a number of other bum cards. She was developmentally disabled, slow to learn and intellectually stunted. Even as an adult, her comprehension and vocabulary skills would never advance beyond those of a sixth-grader. She was also prone to obesity, suffered fits of epilepsy, and had an extremely short fuse which saw her explode into violence at any hint of annoyance. Even to a man as dominant as Thomas Slaughter, she proved impossible to control. It was therefore decided to put her up for adoption.

It was a couple named Falling that drew the short straw and were assigned as adoptive parents. The Fallings had long wanted children of their own and decided that Christine and her younger sister would be perfect. But all too soon they learned that their adopted children were no ordinary girls. They were violent and abusive, surly, insolent and impossible to get through to. The Fallings tried gamely for a time but eventually admitted defeat and sent the girls to a children's home. Christine was nine years old and would remain at the home until the age of 12. During that time, she developed another worrying behavior, one that is commonly found in the backgrounds of serial killers. She began torturing and killing animals, strangling cats to "show them her love," and dropping them from high buildings to see if they really did have nine lives.

One has to wonder at the wisdom of releasing such a violent youngster from custodial care. Nonetheless, after three years at the home, Christine was sent to live with her birth mother in Blountstown, Florida. And if Ann had been unable to control the younger Christine, she had no chance now. The 12-year-old had the run of the house, coming and going as she pleased. Like her mother before her, she had a precocious interest in sex. At fourteen, she married a man in his twenties. The marriage was a near mirror image of the one between her parents and soon fell apart. Christine then returned to live with her mother. Soon she was showing signs of another mental illness, Munchausen Syndrome, a disorder that causes the sufferer to seek medical attention for imagined ailments. Christine soon became a familiar sight at the nearby hospital where she complained of a wide spectrum of ailments, ranging from vaginal bleeding to snakebite. These always turned out to be false.

Christine Falling was by now in her mid-teens, a hulking, disheveled young woman who quite obviously was not in full possession of her mental faculties. Yet, as remarkable as it may seem, there were mothers in Blountstown who were prepared to leave their children in her care. She had, in fact, gained a reputation as a reliable babysitter, one who had a rapport with children and who seemed genuinely to love them. What these trusting parents didn't know was that the smiling Christine who arrived for her babysitting assignments was a quite different persona to the one that emerged after they had departed. Then Falling would begin hurting the children left in her care, pinching, strangling and suffocating, careful always not to leave a mark. Inevitably, though, she pushed things too far.

On February 28, 1980, Falling called 911 and reported that the two-year-old she was babysitting had stopped breathing. Paramedics rushed to the scene but by the time they arrived, Cassidy Johnson was already dead. At first, it was thought that the little girl had died of encephalitis but after an autopsy revealed that the child had suffered a severe skull injury, Falling was pulled in for questioning. Now she changed her story, saying that the baby had somehow managed to pull herself over the safety rail and had fallen from the crib. The police didn't believe her but they were unable to prove otherwise and so Falling walked free.

Babysitting jobs were Christine Falling's sole source of income. And since they had dried up in Blountstown after the death of Cassidy Johnson, Falling decamped to Lakeland, Florida, where she began advertising her services as a child minder. Assignments were quick in coming and in their wake, inevitably, death followed.

In April 1980, four-year-old Jeffrey Davis died while in Christine Falling's care. According to Falling, the boy had suddenly stopped breathing and an autopsy provided at least some validation for that claim. Jeffrey was found to have a rare heart complaint that could, under certain circumstances, cause inflammation. However, the condition is rarely fatal and so medical examiners kept searching for some explanation for the infant's death. Finding none, they declared the death to be natural, under the catch all phrase "heart failure." The case was then closed. That decision would have tragic consequences for another little boy.

Three days after Jeffrey Davis' tragic death, his bereaved aunt and uncle employed Falling to care for their two-year-old son while they attended Jeffrey's funeral. Joseph Spring had, up until that point, seemed like a normal, healthy boy. Exposed to the tender mercies of Christine Falling, however, the child inexplicably died while taking a nap.

A second child had now died in Falling's care within the space of three days and the families, not to mention the local police, were anxious for an explanation. It was not long in coming. The children's physician speculated that Joseph might have succumbed to a viral infection and that the same mysterious disease may have also accounted for Jeffrey Davis. An autopsy might have put the issue beyond doubt but none was ordered. As a result, there was no investigation and Falling walked away scot-free. Shortly afterwards, she left the area and moved to Perry, Florida.

Christine Falling, as we have already noted, was hardly the smartest individual. But even she must have known that the death other another child in her care would not be so easily passed off. And so she traded her childminder gig for that of a caregiver for the elderly. Her first client was 77-year-old Wilbur Swindle and he did not live long. On Falling's first day on the job, Swindle suddenly collapsed and died in his kitchen. Due to his old age and deteriorating health, no suspicions were raised.

Soon after Wilbur Swindle's death, Falling accompanied her stepsister on a shopping trip. Also in the car that day was Falling's eight-month-old niece, Jennifer Daniels, who the young mother made the grave error of leaving in Falling's care while she went into the supermarket. She returned to find Falling in a state of panic and the baby dead. According to Falling, the child had simply stopped breathing.

One might have thought that authorities would have paid greater scrutiny to yet another child death involving Christine Falling. But the autopsy ruled the death to be from natural causes and so there was no inquiry. Christine Falling was free to kill again and a year later she claimed another victim.

Travis Coleman was only ten weeks old on the night in June 1982, when his parents left him in Falling's care and returned to find him dead. Questioned by police, Falling spun her familiar tale. The boy had suddenly stopped breathing for no reason, she said. This time, however, the autopsy would tell a different story. According to the medical examiner, Travis had been suffocated.

Now the police leaned hard on Falling, demanding the truth about the child's death. And the dim-witted Christine did not hold up long under such fierce interrogation. She admitted that she'd killed Travis Coleman, then confessed that she'd also murdered three other children by what she described as "smotheration." She claimed that she'd heard voices ordering her to kill the children by placing a blanket over their faces. "I don't know why I done what I done," she said. "The way I done it, I seen it done on TV shows. I had my own way, though. Simple and easy. No one would hear them scream."

Christine Falling was found guilty of three counts of murder and sentenced to life imprisonment, with the stipulation that she must serve 25 years before she becomes eligible for parole. At time of writing, she remains behind bars.

Catherine Flannagan & Margaret Higgins

The slum districts of Liverpool, England were a truly dreadful place to live during the 1800's. Row upon row of squalid tenement houses lined the filth-strewn streets, each residence crammed to the brim with forlorn, poverty-stricken people. It was a place where entire families occupied a single small room, where one toilet served the whole road, where houses had no plumbing and residents were forced to queue for water at a solitary fountain in the street. Filth and disease were everywhere and mortality rates, especially among the very young and the elderly were extremely high. Still, one house on Skirving Street seems to have been the scene of so many unexplained deaths that even in these horrendous conditions it drew attention.

Number 5 Skirving Street was the home of Catherine Flannagan and her sister Margaret Thompson. Maggie and Catty (as they were known to neighbors) were both of Irish descent and had come to Liverpool in the late 1840's to escape the Irish Potato Famine. Like many of their countrymen, they'd chosen to remain once the famine was over. By 1880, Catherine was the landlady at 5 Skirving Street while Margaret was working as a charlady. Both women were widows with a reputation for drunkenness and dishonesty. The other residents at 5 Skirving Street at this time were: Thomas Higgins and his daughter Mary aged 8; Patrick Jennings and his 16-year-old daughter Margaret; and John Flannagan, Catherine's 22-year-old son.

John Flannagan was quite unlike his mother. While Catherine was known for her aggressive disposition and propensity for violence when drunk, John was universally liked in the neighborhood for his friendly and outgoing nature. He worked as a laborer and the physical demands of that trade had chiseled him into a strapping young man who seldom, if ever, missed a day of work. Everyone was surprised when he fell ill from a mystery ailment in December 1880 and had to be confined to bed. Everyone that is, except his mother. She'd been saying for weeks that she didn't expect him to see out the year.

And that prediction turned out to be correct. Just short of Christmas 1880, John Flannagan was released from his agonizing death throes. His mother, who had attended him throughout his short illness promptly cashed in the £70 policy she'd taken out on his life and set off for the nearest tavern, where she got falling down drunk. She'd continue her boozing binge over the weeks that followed. People could accept that, they figured that Catherine was drinking to numb the pain of losing her son. What they couldn't understand was why, despite her generous insurance payout, she had spent just a few shillings to bury John in a pauper's grave?

A year passed. By 1882, a romance had sprung up between Margaret Thompson and lodger Thomas Higgins and in October of that year they married. But the marriage was soon tainted by tragedy. Just a month after the nuptials, Thomas' daughter Mary became ill, her condition marked by stomach cramps, vomiting and diarrhea. Within days, Mary was dead and her new stepmother wasted no time in redeeming the £22 burial policy she'd just purchased on the little girl. No suspicion seems to have been aroused by the fact that Mary's symptoms were remarkably similar to those of John Flannagan.

But the next death to occur at 5 Skirving Road did get the tongues wagging. In January 1883, 16-year-old Margaret Jennings died suddenly of symptoms that bore the hallmarks of both John and Mary's illnesses. Still, neighbors might have let that pass had Catherine Flannagan not benefitted from the death. Although not related to Margaret Jennings, she'd taken out a policy on the girl's life and with her £50 windfall in hand she hit the taverns and started drinking hard, causing outrage among some of her Skirving Street neighbors. A number of angry confrontations resulted during which Catherine was accused outright of murder. Perhaps fearful that these utterings might reach the ears of the authorities, the sisters decided that a change of scene might be appropriate. They didn't go far. Just to nearby Latimer Street and shortly thereafter to a basement apartment at 27 Ascot Street. And wherever they set up home, death inevitably followed.

In September 1883, Thomas Higgins began suffering severe stomach cramps. A doctor was called and diagnosed his illness as dysentery, a common consequence of drinking the cheap whiskey sold in local pubs at the time. The doctor prescribed opium and castor oil but it was to no avail. Thomas died in extreme pain two days later. The following day his widow visited five different burial societies, scooping up £100 in insurance payouts.

But on this occasion, the sisters had overstepped the mark. Thomas' brother Patrick was suspicious of his sibling's sudden death and had reason to recall a conversation they'd had weeks earlier. Thomas had told him that an insurance agent had turned up at the house with a doctor, wanting to examine him in order to write a burial policy. Thomas had told them that he wasn't about to die and had thrown them out.

Patrick Higgins now began making the rounds of the local insurance companies and soon learned that his brother's life had been insured with several of them. He next visited the doctor who had signed the death certificate and asked him whether Thomas might have been poisoned. The doctor admitted that it was possible and then agreed to accompany Patrick to report the matter to the police.

On the day that Thomas Higgins was to be buried, a coroner arrived at 27 Ascot Street in the company of a couple of burly constables. They found a raucous wake in progress, with several inebriated women cavorting around the open coffin. On seeing the officers, Catherine Flannagan gave a cry of alarm and bolted out the back door. The coroner then informed Margaret Higgins that there was to be a postmortem. That examination would prove conclusively that Thomas Higgins had died from arsenic poisoning.

Margaret was immediately arrested while Catherine remained at large for a week, moving from house to house until she was eventually captured. The police meanwhile had conducted a search of 27 Ascot Street and found a quantity of liquid arsenic (believed to have been distilled from flypaper) as well as traces of the poison on Margaret Higgins' clothing.

The bodies of John Flannagan, Margaret Jennings and Mary Higgins were then exhumed. Each bore lethal doses of arsenic.

Faced with the incontrovertible evidence against her, Catherine Flannagan turned on her younger sister and offered to testify against her in exchange for a more lenient sentence. That offer was immediately rejected.

Flannagan then tried another tack, offering to provide the authorities with details of a broader murder-for-profit scheme involving at least 17 murders. According to Flannagan, the conspirators were all women and included three other poisoners – who she named as her sister Margaret, plus Margaret Evans and Bridget Begley. Three more women – Margaret Potter, Bridget Stanton and Emily Fallon – had written the insurance policies. Another, Catherine Ryan, was allegedly responsible for obtaining the arsenic.

Ultimately, Flannagan's desperate plea to strike a deal would fail. The Prosecuting Solicitor for Liverpool decided that while there was undoubtedly some truth to her confession, it would be impossible to prove murder in the 17 deaths she had cited. Flannagan and Higgins' co-conspirators were off the hook. They, however, would have to answer for their crimes.

The sisters went on trial at St George's Hall on February 14, 1884, charged with only one murder, that of Thomas Higgins. Three days later, the jury deliberated for just 40 minutes before delivering a guilty verdict. The judge then donned the black cap and passed sentence of death.

Catherine Flannagan and Margaret Higgins were hanged side by side at Liverpool's Kirkdale Prison on March 3, 1884. Over one thousand people braved a fierce snowstorm to see them put to death.

Elizabeth Duncan

It was one of the most sensational criminal cases in California history, the brutal murder of a pretty young nurse, 7 months pregnant at the time, by a couple of bungling assassins, hired for the task by the victim's mother-in-law. As if that wasn't enough, there were the other astonishing aspects of the case, the intensely jealous mother-in-law, the 29-year-old "mama's boy" who walked away from his pregnant wife to return to her clutches; the question of incest between them. It was a tragedy of Shakespearean proportions, one that would ultimately result in the deaths of four of the players.

Elizabeth Duncan was an unconventional woman. Besides being a contender for the worst mother-in-law in history, she was also a ruthless con artist running a well-worked scam. This involved the 54-year-old Duncan persuading numerous young men to marry her. She did this by convincing the men that she was about to come into a sizable inheritance but could only claim it if she was married. If he played along, she'd say, she'd cut him in on a tidy commission, after which they could get a quickie divorce. There was, of course, no inheritance. Her objective was to steal as much from her new husband as possible and then nail him for alimony once the divorce went through. Running this scheme, Duncan was married and divorced at least eleven times.

Yet despite all these marriages, Elizabeth had only two children, a daughter named Patricia and a son named Frank, the apple of her eye. By all accounts, Frank Duncan was an intelligent and well-adjusted young man. But his relationship with his mother was incredibly unhealthy, perhaps even incestuous (this was suggested in the media at the time of the trial although never stated implicitly and never proven).

In 1956, Frank Duncan was 27 years old and had just qualified as a lawyer. That same year, he and his mother moved together to Santa Barbara, California, where Frank began his career at law. For her part, Elizabeth attended all of his court days. When Frank won a case or even if he brought across a good point, she was on her feet applauding as though she'd just viewed a brilliant piece of theater. If any of these antics embarrassed Frank, he gave no inkling.

What did get to Frank, though, were the jibes of his former college mates. They suggested that he should "be a man" and break free of his mother. Frank appears to have taken this advice on board because he began standing up to Elizabeth more and more, even going out on dates, which he knew infuriated her. It all came to a head in 1957 when, after an argument that turned violent, he ordered Elizabeth to move out of his apartment. She responded in typically melodramatic fashion, swallowing a handful of sleeping tablets and ending up in the hospital to have her stomach pumped. In this simple occurrence, the seeds of tragedy were planted.

While Elizabeth was in the hospital, she was attended by a pretty 29-year-old nurse named Olga Kupczyk. Frank, who had by now come scurrying back to his mother's side, visited her often during her convalescence. During these visits, he began paying more and more attention to Olga, spending as much time with her as he did with his mother. Eventually, he plucked up the courage to ask her out and Olga said yes. Elizabeth's worst nightmare had come true. She was faced with the very real possibility of losing her son to another woman.

Not that Elizabeth was giving up without a fight. Over the next three months, she phoned Olga daily and threatened her to leave her son alone or else. On one occasion, when Olga told her that she and Frank were going to be married, Elizabeth replied, "You'll never marry my son. I'll kill you first."

But Frank and Olga did marry, albeit in secret on June 20, 1958.

To keep up the pretense, Frank continued to live with his mother, only visiting his new bride in her apartment intermittently. On one of those occasions, Elizabeth followed him and banged on the door demanding that he come home with her. Ever the dutiful son, Frank followed her home like a scolded puppy.

But a few days later, Frank appears to have finally acquired some backbone. Renting a new apartment, he moved in with Olga, keeping the location secret from his mother. Elizabeth was apoplectic. In the middle of July 1958, she told Barbara Reed, an old friend, that Olga was pregnant by another man and was duping Frank into believing that the child was his. She then shocked Mrs. Reed by offering her $1,500 to help her kill Olga. Mrs. Reed said that she'd think about it. Instead, she told Frank of the proposal his mother had made. His response was unusual, to say the least. Rather than confront his mother about the allegation, he moved back into her home.

Her beloved Frank was now back under her roof, but he was still married to Olga and Elizabeth wouldn't allow that to stand. Early in August 1958, she enlisted an ex-con named Ralph Winterstein to help her carry out a scam. The plan was to annul the marriage between Frank and Olga and to this extent, the pair appeared before a judge, with Elizabeth posing as Olga and Winterstein as Frank. The "annulment" was granted after Winterstein testified that his wife had never lived with him and refused to do so. Still not satisfied, Elizabeth tried to recruit Winterstein to kill Olga. He refused, but failed to report the matter to the police.

Winterstein's refusal, however, had not discouraged Elizabeth from the murderous thoughts percolating in her brain. Over the months that followed she approached four other people, seeking help to get rid of Olga. The first was a friend, Diane Romero, who refused. She then tried Romero's husband Rudolph, but he too turned her down. Next, she approached Rebecca Diaz, who owned the house the Romeros lived in. She asked Diaz if she knew of a man who could "get Olga out of town." Diaz agreed to let her know if she heard of anyone.

Eventually, on November 12, 1958, Elizabeth turned to Esperanza Esquivel, owner of the Tropical Cafe in Santa Barbara. Esquivel was a client of Frank's and she owed him a debt of gratitude for getting her an acquittal in a criminal case. Playing on that, Elizabeth told her that Olga had threatened to throw acid in Frank's face. Esquivel then said that she might know someone who'd be interested. She asked Elizabeth to come back the following day.

When Elizabeth did return, there were two men waiting to meet her, Luis Moya and Gus Baldonado, aged 21 and 26 respectively. Details were discussed and it was agreed that Elizabeth would pay $3,000 on completion of the job and another $3,000 within six months. The plan was for Moya and Baldonado to kidnap Olga, drive her over the border into Mexico and kill her in Tijuana. In order to carry it out, the assassins said they needed $175 for transportation and a gun. Elizabeth asked them to wait and left the cantina. She returned with the money a short while later, having obtained it by pawning her jewelry.

The murder was now set in motion. There was no stopping it.

At around midnight on November 17, 1958, there was a knock on the door of Olga Duncan's Santa Barbara apartment. Olga, by now seven months pregnant, opened the door to a young man who seemed quite agitated. He told her that her husband, Frank Duncan, was drunk in a car downstairs and that he needed her help to bring Frank up to the apartment. Olga had not seen Frank since he'd packed up his things and moved back in with his mother 10 days earlier, but she was worried about him.

Pulling on her robe, she followed the man (Moya) to the car. There, Baldonado sat crouched over, pretending to be Frank. As Olga leaned into the vehicle to see her husband, Moya struck her on the back of the head with the butt of the pistol. Simultaneously, Baldonado grabbed her and pulled her into the back seat.

But Olga was not knocked unconscious, and she was stronger than either of the thugs had anticipated. She began to kick and scream, whereupon the men continued clubbing her with the weapon and with their fists until they eventually knocked her out. They then bound her hands with tape.

With their victim now subdued, the killers headed south on Highway 101. But it was soon clear that the 1948 Chevrolet sedan they had "hired" from a friend for $25 wasn't going to make it to the border. Just outside of Carpinteria, they decided on a new plan, turned onto Casitas Pass Road and headed into Ventura County.

Olga Duncan came to several times during the journey and was each time pistol-whipped back into unconsciousness. Eventually, the gun disintegrated under the force of the blows. A short while later, Moya pulled the car to a halt and the killers got out, hauled Olga from the car and dragged her down an embankment.

The gun, of course, had been rendered useless for its intended purpose so the men took turns strangling Olga, until Baldonado, who had served as an Army medic, decided that she was dead. They then dug a shallow grave and dropped Olga into it. An autopsy would later reveal that she'd been buried alive.

Baldonado and Moya headed back to Santa Barbara, where they hid their bloody clothes and ripped out the blood-soaked seat covers of the car. They told their friend that the covers had been burned by a cigarette and promised to pay for repairs. They were, of course, expecting a big windfall.

However, when it came time for Elizabeth to make good on her part of the deal, she told them that she couldn't take any money out of her bank account because the police were suspicious about Olga's disappearance. As a good-faith gesture, she gave them $150, money Frank had given her to buy a typewriter.

A few days later, Frank queried his mother about the money. Put on the spot, Elizabeth said that she had given it to two men who were blackmailing her, naming Moya and Baldonado. Frank Duncan then made the fateful decision to report the "blackmail" to the police and in so doing brought down the entire house of cards that his mother had constructed.

In short order, Moya and Baldonado were arrested. Under interrogation, they denied blackmail but then made the stunning admission that they had been hired by Elizabeth Duncan to kill her daughter-in-law. On December 21, they led investigators to Olga's makeshift grave. That same day, all three of the conspirators were indicted for murder.

At her trial, Duncan insisted that she'd had no involvement in Olga's murder and that Moya and Baldonado had acted alone in carrying out the crime. As the two assassins had not even known Olga before the night they'd abducted her, this was never going to fly. Found guilty of murder all three conspirators were sentenced to death.

The date of execution was set for August 8, 1962. Moya and Baldanado went first, strapped side by side as they inhaled the noxious fumes in California's gas chamber.

Then it was Elizabeth Duncan's turn. As she was led into the chamber, she scanned the room frantically for her son. He wasn't there. He was at the federal courthouse, trying desperately to win a last-minute reprieve for the woman who had killed his wife and unborn child. Elizabeth Duncan's final words were reportedly, "Where's Frank?"

Marilyn Plantz

To the outside world, Jim and Marilyn Plantz seemed like an ordinary, happily married couple. He was an assistant press supervisor at the Daily Oklahoman newspaper, working the night shift. She was a stay-at-home mom. Both were devoted to their children, Trina, 9, and Christopher, 6. Neighbors liked them, especially Jim, who was described as an easy-going, fun-loving guy.

But peel back the curtain of this suburban bliss and a somewhat different picture emerged. The couple, who had married when Marilyn was just 16, were constantly at each other's throats. Most of the fights were initiated by Marilyn, who was bored with being a housewife and child minder and was not afraid to let Jim know it. Several times she threatened to walk out on the marriage to which Jim responded that he would kill himself if she left him. Whether it was that threat or love for her children that kept Marilyn from leaving, nobody knows. But stay she did, at least notionally.

What Jim Plantz and his neighbors in Midwest City did not know, was that Marilyn was living a double life. Every evening, just after Jim pulled away from the family home, heading for his night shift, Marilyn would bundle Trina and Christopher into her car and drive away. The children went to a babysitter. Marilyn went to a local park where she worked as a prostitute to fund her drug habit. She also had a teenaged lover, an 18-year-old delinquent named William Clifford Bryson. It was to him that she first floated the idea of murdering her husband.

At first, Bryson wanted nothing to do with the plan. The prospect of shacking up with Marilyn was an appealing one, but when you factored in her two kids, as well as the painful truth that neither he nor Marilyn had any legitimate way of earning a living, it appeared less so. The prospect of two fat insurance policies sweetened the deal. "Three hundred thousand dollars," Marilyn whispered in her lover's ear. "That's what he's worth dead."

At the mention of money, Bryson was suddenly all ears. "I'll need some help," he said after a moment's contemplation. "I know just the right guy."

The "right guy," as it turned out was Roderick Farris, street name Popeye, an acquaintance of Bryson. He agreed to meet with Marilyn the next day, after Bryson spun him a tall tale about Marilyn's abusive husband and how he regularly used her as a punching bag.

The following evening, Bryson and Farris arrived at Marilyn's home after Jim had left for work. The threesome spent some time negotiating a price before $10,000 was agreed as Farris' fee. Then they got down to talking about the murder itself, with Marilyn insisting that it had to look like an accident. She suggested that Bryson and Farris follow her husband the next time he went fishing, and then drown him in the lake. It was perfect, she chuckled, because everyone knew that Jim couldn't swim.

Perfect it may have been, but Farris decided then and there that he wanted no part of it. He didn't like the way Bryson and Marilyn kissed and cuddled while talking about killing a man in cold blood. He didn't like the way Marilyn giggled while negotiating the death of the father of her children. Most of all, he didn't like being the third wheel on this particular wagon. If things went south, Bryson and Marilyn were likely to gang up and put the blame on him.

Farris left the house after turning down the $10,000 bounty offered by Marilyn Plantz. Later that night, he was arrested while trying to steal a truck. By the time the murder took place, he'd be safely locked up in prison – the perfect alibi.

The next person Bryson turned to for help was a fellow delinquent named Clinton McKimble. Unlike Roderick Farris, 18-year-old McKimble had no scruples about killing a man for money. He wasn't about to do it on the cheap, though. His price was $45,000. After some back and forth, Marilyn eventually agreed to pay. "After all," she reasoned. "You can't put a price on freedom."

And so a date was set and a plan was agreed. The idea was that Bryson and McKimble would gun down Jim Plantz on his way home from work. To this extent, Marilyn even provided them with a weapon, a double-barreled shotgun that she stole from her husband's gun cabinet.

On a stormy night in early August 1988, Bryson and McKimble waited in a car outside the printing works of the Daily Oklahoman. Despite the hour, the air was hot and sticky, with intermittent showers driven by swirling winds. Just before 4 a.m., Bryson spotted Jim's pickup. He poked his companion in the ribs and pointed out the vehicle. "That's him," he said and started the car, pulling it away from the curb as Jim Plantz passed them. McKimble, sitting in the passenger seat with the shotgun across his knees, twitched nervously.

The rain had picked up while the killers were waiting for Plantz. It made visibility difficult. Bryson gunned the engine and began overtaking the truck. His plan was to cut in front of Plantz, forcing him to a stop. But before he could do that, another vehicle appeared out of the rain, driving in the opposite direction. Bryson stood on the brakes and veered his vehicle left, bringing it to a shuddering halt and stalling it on the slick blacktop. By the time he got the vehicle started again, Jim Plantz was out of sight.

Marilyn was annoyed that Bryson and McKimble hadn't carried through with the plan. But Bryson reassured her that it was a temporary hiccup. "We'll get him next time," he said. "I've got a new plan. And this one won't fail."

In the early hours of August 26, 1988, while Jim Plantz was working his night shift, Marilyn ushered Bryson and McKimble into her house. The three of them snorted cocaine and drank beer together before passing out on the couch. At around 3:40 am, Marilyn shook Bryson awake. "It's time," she said, handing him a baseball bat belonging to her son, Christopher. Then she dropped another bat next to the still-sleeping form of McKimble and retired to bed.

By 4:20, Bryson and McKimble were crouching in the darkened living room when they heard Jim Plantz's pickup pull into the driveway. A short while later, they heard him walking up the path, then turning his key in the lock. Jim stepped into the passage and walked towards the kitchen, carrying a bag of groceries in each hand. He'd just stepped into the living room when Bryson and McKimble attacked.

Caught totally by surprise, Plantz had no chance. Blow after blow rained down on him, buckling his knee, breaking an arm that he threw up to protect himself. As he fell to the ground, one of his assailants swung at his head, shattering his jaw. "Marilyn!" Plantz screamed in agony. But he'd get no help from her. Marilyn was lying in bed with a pillow clutched to her chest, listening to her husband being beaten to death in the home where they'd raised their children. Eventually, when Jim's cries died down and all that could be heard was the dull thud of the bats striking flesh, she got up and walked to the living room. The scene that greeted her there caused her to suck in a sharp intake of breath.

"You idiots!" Marilyn shouted at her accomplices. "You were supposed to make this look like an accident! How are we going to pass this off as an accident?"

"I thought we could put him in his car," Bryson said. "Push it off the road. Make it look like an auto wreck."

"With those welts on his body? The cops would see through that in five seconds flat." She paused for a moment contemplating the next move. "We're going to have to burn him," she said.

To the addle-brained threesome, the plan seemed foolproof. Put Jim in his truck, drive him to a secluded road and set the truck on fire. It would look like he'd lost control of his vehicle in the wet conditions and run off the road. The truck had then impacted with something, which had caused the gas tank to explode, cooking the unfortunate man in his seat.

While Bryson and McKimble dragged Jim out to the truck, Marilyn got busy cleaning up the blood-drenched crime scene. She had to work fast. Her children would be up soon. Bryson and McKimble, meanwhile, drove to an isolated stretch of woodland in eastern Oklahoma County. There, they positioned Jim's body behind the steering wheel, doused it and the truck with gasoline and threw a match. It was then, as the flames ignited in a whoosh of hot air, that Jim Plantz regained consciousness.

The killers, who had believed that their victim was dead, watched in horror as he grabbed the steering wheel and pulled himself upright. Then his arms began thrashing violently, as he desperately fought to escape the burning cab. It was no use. The flames quickly overwhelmed him. Soon the air was filled with the sickening barbecue stench of seared flesh. By the time Bryson and

McKimble left the scene, driving away in Marilyn's station wagon, all that remained of Jim Plantz was a blackened stump, barely recognizable as human.

Jim's body was found an hour later, after a passerby summoned firefighters to the scene of the smoldering wreck. The police were also called and it didn't take them long to figure out that Jim Plantz had met with foul play. Identifying the victim from the license plate of his vehicle, officers went to his home. When she was told of her husband's death, Marilyn turned in an Oscar-worthy performance, collapsing to the ground and sobbing pitifully. Once she had sufficiently recovered her composure, she began making tearful calls to friends and relatives, sharing the terrible news.

But despite her over-the-top show of emotion (or perhaps because of it), Marilyn was never far from the top of the suspect list. The police quickly learned that she stood to gain handsomely from her husband's death, and by Monday, August 28, she was placed under arrest and charged with murder. It did not take long before she gave up the names of her accomplices. Within hours, Bill Bryson and Clinton McKimble were also in custody. Then Marilyn changed her story, claiming she had nothing to do with Jim's death, and that Bryson had acted alone to get rid of his rival in love. It might even have worked had the D.A. not offered McKimble a deal in exchange for his testimony against his co-accused.

McKimble accepted a life sentence, thus avoiding the death penalty that the prosecution was seeking for Marilyn Plantz and Bill Bryson. At the March 1989 trial, McKimble described in detail how he and Bryson had ambushed Jim Plantz in the living room, how they'd beaten him to a pulp, how they'd set him alight thinking he was dead. He made it clear that the primary mover in the murder plot was Marilyn. That assertion was given credence by the testimony of Roderick Farris, the original assassin Marilyn and Bryson had tried to hire.

It took the jury less than three hours to find the deadly pair guilty of murder and less than five more to opt for the death penalty. Thereafter, they were moved to separate prisons to await their respective dates with the executioner.

William Bryson went first. His appeals exhausted, he was put to death by lethal injection on July 16, 2000. Then, on May 1, 2001, it was the turn of Marilyn Plantz. She had in the interim become a born again Christian and had reconciled with her daughter. Yet she made no attempt to apologize for her actions, choosing instead to quote from the Bible in her final statement. She became only the seventh woman executed in the United States since the reinstatement of the death penalty. Most would argue that it was a fate she richly deserved.

For more True Crime books by Robert Keller please visit

http://bit.ly/kellerbooks

23090489R00094

Printed in Poland
by Amazon Fulfillment
Poland Sp. z o.o., Wrocław